PROGRAMMED LEARNING:
Theory and Research

An Enduring Problem in Psychology

SELECTED READINGS

Edited by
WENDELL I. SMITH
Bucknell University

AND

J. WILLIAM MOORE
Bucknell University

AN INSIGHT BOOK

D. VAN NOSTRAND COMPANY, INC.
PRINCETON, NEW JERSEY

TORONTO   LONDON

NEW YORK

D. VAN NOSTRAND COMPANY, INC.
120 Alexander St., Princeton, New Jersey
(*Principal Office*)
24 West 40 Street, New York 18, New York

D. VAN NOSTRAND COMPANY, LTD.
358, Kensington High Street, London, W.14, England

D. VAN NOSTRAND COMPANY (Canada), LTD.
25 Hollinger Road, Toronto 16, Canada

Published simultaneously in Canada by
D. VAN NOSTRAND COMPANY (Canada), LTD.

Foreword
By the Editors of the Series

In the field of psychology we believe that the student ought to get the "feel" of experimentation by reading original source materials. In this way he can acquire a better understanding of the discipline by seeing scientific ideas grow and change. However, one of the main problems in teaching is the limited availability of these sources, which communicate most effectively the personality of the author and the excitement of ongoing research.

For these reasons we have decided to edit several books,* each devoted to a particular problem in psychology. In every case we attempt to select problems that have been and are controversial—that have been and still are alive. We intend to present these problems as a set of selected original articles, arranged in historical order and in order of progress in the field. We believe that it is important for the student to see that theories and researches build on what has gone before; that one study leads to another, that theory leads to research and then to revision of theory. We believe that *telling* the student this does not make the same kind of impression as letting him see it happen in actuality. The idea is for the student to read and build ideas for himself.

Suggestions for Use—These readings books can be used by the student in either of two ways. They are organized so that, with the help of the instructor (or of the students if used in seminars), a topic can be covered at length and in depth. This would necessitate lectures or discussions on articles not covered in the series to fill in the gaps. On the other hand, each book taken alone will give a student a good idea of the problem being covered and its historical background as well as its present state and the direction it seems to be taking.

---

* (Pub. note: a sub-series within the Insight Book Series.)

Preface

The field of programmed learning, or auto-instructional materials (erroneously called "teaching machines"), is a rapidly developing, extremely exciting movement toward the further development of an instructional technology based, in part, on certain principles of psychology derived from laboratory studies of human and animal learning which serve to confirm, in part, the procedures and techniques used by nearly all truly great teachers of the past.

Many professions other than psychology have a legitimate interest in instructional technology, e.g., specialists in the fields of audio-visual materials, curriculum development, engineering, systems development, teacher education, educational administration, and communications. This set of readings concerns itself with only a small part of the field of instructional technology, programmed learning, and it stresses that material of greatest interest to psychologists, particularly educational psychologists. Only in the first article, Finn's "A New Theory of Instructional Technology," will the reader find the broad concern with this topic. Finn's article represents, then, the broad context within which one might view some of the work of several professions, including psychology.

Psychology's concern with an instructional technology is rather recent, and it has been limited chiefly to evaluative studies of media. Its interest in programmed learning and auto-instructional devices is far greater than its interest in other media, since two psychologists, B. F. Skinner and Sidney L. Pressey, have been the pioneers in the development of self-teaching devices and materials. Beginning with Skinner's 1954 paper entitled "The Science of Learning and the Art of Teaching," psychology's claim to a contribution to developing an instructional technology gained considerable support. In a sense, Skinner proposed that laboratory studies of animal learning serve as a base for a science of teaching; however, earlier work with human learning is not to be considered irrelevant to the developments in programming. The work of Ebbinghaus and his followers, of Thorndike and his students and of Pressey and his students inevitably bears a relationship to programmed learning.

A casual perusal by a humanist of the rapidly growing literature on self-instructional devices and programmed material would probably give rise to either the fantasies of *Alice in Wonderland* and the *Wizard of Oz* or a vision of *Brave New World*, *Walden Two* and *1984*. These views of the field, however, are quite inaccurate, as one can discover by critical reading of those articles prepared within a scholarly tradition rather than of those prepared within the frame-of-reference of technology and commercialism. Unfortunately, much of the activity in this area has been concerned with the development of machines rather than with the development of materials for use with or without machines. Well over one hundred programs are being developed and, as a consequence, the respective roles of machines and programs will become clearer within a few years.

Until programmed material is available in reasonable amounts, it is difficult to engage in research on the many variables which are of great interest to psychologists. Perhaps it might be said that one of the most exciting possibilities before us is an opportunity for the first time to conduct research on the human learning of continuous discourse material with reasonable experimental control over the instructor variable. Machines are impartial, impersonal, and uniform. Teachers, fortunately, are personal and individual, but these desirable qualities frequently have been confounding variables in educational research on teaching methods and the parameters of learning under classroom or field conditions. The number of studies on variables operating in programmed learning is increasing rapidly, and soon there will be data to support or refute the many claims which have been made.

Our selection of the readings was guided by the several considerations set forth in the preceding paragraphs. The development and an overview of the field and some of the relevant psychological theory are presented in Part I, the method—programming—is presented in Part II, and samples of research based on the methods of programming are presented in Part III. The nature of teaching machines or auto-instructional devices has been minimized deliberately in the selection of readings on the grounds that at the present stage of development of the field, the *method* for testing the most promising psychology theory for a science of teaching is the *program* which may or may not require a machine for presentation of the program content. Therefore, descriptions and functions of machines will be found only as integral parts of articles, the primary concern of which is programming as a method or research on the parameters of learning from programmed material.

Each new development in science tends to generate its own vocabulary, and this is particularly true of an interdisciplinary subject like programmed learning. To help those readers who are unfamiliar with the particular terminolgy which has developed for this area, a glossary of teaching machine terms is given in Appendix A.

For those readers who are interested in specific information on some of the existing machines and programs, Appendix B provides the names and addresses of several machine manufacturers and program distributors. Additional information on most of the topics discussed in this book can be found in other publications, a list of which is also provided in Appendix B.

Contents

Part I

EDITOR'S NOTE

The set of articles reprinted in this section was selected to define the problem and to present some of the issues and the background for them. The educational problem which has given rise to the great interest in teaching machines and programming is ably presented by James Finn who has long been a leader in audio-visual education. The articles by B. F. Skinner and James Holland describe the theory and research in psychology upon which much of the recent work on programmed learning has been based. A somewhat different theoretical framework for programmed learning will be found in David Zeaman's article.

Professor Fry's article attempts to define an issue which perhaps has had more attention than it warrants, viz., whether the mode of response is a critical variable in learning via programmed material.

A thorough, thoughtful and valuable review of the work on teaching machines and programming from a psychologist's view is provided for the purpose of bridging theory, method, and research.

I

A New Theory for Instructional Technology*

JAMES D. FINN

University of Southern California

Technology[1] relates to education in at least three major ways. First, in a society in which science and technology are primary, such as America, the society requires that the educational system insure an adequate supply of scientists and associated technicians. This requirement sets a curriculum problem, an organization problem, and many other problems associated with the screening, selection, and education of young people as potential additions to the nation's technical manpower.

Second, as a society becomes more and more technologically oriented and controlled, the question of the general education of all citizens is raised. The survival and management of the whole society theoretically require more general education in the sciences and tech-

* This article was reprinted from *Audio Visual Communication Review*, 1960, **8**, 84-94. It is used here with the permission of the author.

[1] For purposes of this paper, no distinction is made between "science" and "technology" or between "pure" and "applied" science. The distinction between "basic" and "applied" research is perhaps more meaningful, but these two activities are still regarded here as positions on a continuum. From a societal point of view, it matters little whether the society is hit with new ideas or new processes that stem from the ideas, or, as is more likely, a combination of the two.

nology for all. Pressures arise for more mathematics and science to be taught to the entire population. Again, curriculum problems, organization problems, and a host of nagging, persistent general education problems arise.

Third, because of the tendency for technology to have no limits and constantly to extend into new areas, it is inevitable that, in an advanced technical society, technology should begin to extend into the instructional process itself. As will be shown, this is particularly true when education has been, for a century or more, one of the areas of American society which has walled itself off from technological advances and, consequently, has created a technological vacuum. That vacuum is now rapidly being filled.

It is with this third relationship—the application of technology to the educational, or to be more precise, to the instructional process—that the balance of this paper is concerned. The three relationships just discussed—development of technicians, general education in technology, and the application of technology to the instructional process—cannot eventually be completely separated. However, the third relationship is sufficiently different to merit thorough analysis.

Again for purposes of this paper, a finer distinction will now be drawn. Within the educational process itself, there are three general areas in which technology can or is being applied. These are: (1) general administration, (2) testing, and (3) instruction. The uses of technical management systems, modern equipment, etc., represent the fairly obvious applications to the field of general administration. While it probably can easily be shown that this area of management is, taken as a whole, two or three decades behind its counterpart in industry, the problems associated with technology and school management are not as difficult as some of the others and will not, at this time, be considered. This is not to say that administration is not highly interrelated with the other two areas of testing and instruction, but the position can be taken that the problems arising from the latter two should guide the technical solutions in administration, not the other way around.

The second category, testing, is in many respects the

most highly developed technology at present existing in American education. This is true both from a machine and from a systems standpoint. Further, the close relationships between psychological, achievement, and other types of testing and the instructional process are so well defined as to need no comment. However, with some exceptions, the technology of the instructional process can, for purposes of analysis, be isolated from testing. This arbitrary decision is made here in order to further the remainder of the discussion. We are left, then, with the instructional process by itself and can now turn to the impact of technology upon that process.

DEVELOPMENT OF INSTRUCTIONAL TECHNOLOGY

The development of a technology of the instructional process is relatively new. In the pre-industrial phases of both education and industry, while industry was principally at the handwork, artisan level, the instructional process relied upon such devices as the slate, the hornbook, the blackboard, chalk, and limited single textbooks with few illustrations. Although attention will be confined principally to some of the symbols of technology—equipment and machines—it should be emphasized that other factors were in the same state. In the area of organization, for example, it is well known that the graded school is a late development.

We note the famous changes in industry at the beginning of the 19th century—the invention of a group of related machines for power, spinning, weaving, etc.—which made possible the factory system. Based on the work of Toynbee the elder, the term "Industrial Revolution" is applied to this period.[2] In education, however, the same revolution did *not* occur and instructional technology (with some exceptions here and there) remained at the pre-industrial level. During the last quarter of the century, there was some indication of incipient change. Oliver (1956) notes that an exhibit from an American school "with maps, charts, textbooks and other equipment" won admiration at the International Exposition in Vienna in 1873. He adds that the American

[2] Now called the First Industrial Revolution.

school display at Paris in 1878 was even more outstanding. Significantly, Oliver's last mention of international attention to American instructional technology was at Melbourne in 1880.

By 1900 industry had, in contrast, established factories and was moving into assembly line operations; had begun to apply, in a crude way, research and development concepts; had introduced the beginnings of modern management; and had developed a sophisticated financial system. Developments had reached such a state that the perceptive Henry Adams, true prophet and seer of technology, foretold the coming of the Age of the Atom and the problems it would bring. In the years to 1950, aided by the acceleration of two wars, technology burgeoned and developed, piled machine upon machine, system upon system, added fantastically to its power resources, and invented the method of invention. Technology transformed American society, philosophy, and art.

During the period from 1900 to 1950, however, technology only washed lightly upon the shores of instruction. In this same time span, when high speed printing techniques, radio, sound motion pictures, television, and other pieces of communication technology were invented, developed, and exploited, American education failed to apply these devices in quantity to the instructional process and, of course, failed to develop the appropriate technological systems necessary for this application. There were always rumblings, to be sure, as evidenced by the statement attributed to Edison in 1916 that the motion picture would replace the teacher. However, looked at from the vantage point of 1960, laboratories, project methods, libraries, and minute arrangements for audio-visual materials—the provisions to 1950 constituted what was still a pre-industrial technology for instruction.

By 1950, industry had entered what may be called the pre-automation period, which heralded the beginning of a movement toward true automation. Much of the basic work on computers and other control mechanisms had been done. At this time also, mechanical systems of transporting work goods between machines had integrated some production lines into a system called "Detroit automation." The period of true automation was dawning, and I have arbitrarily set 1955 as the date at which this electronic-mechanical-systems analysis procedure began to be significantly applied. It is no accident that man began to push toward space at about the same time.

By 1950, American education had the potentiality (to carry on with the analogy) of a mass production technology. The hardware—projectors, recorders, television—and the materials were present. The systems concepts—saturation with audiovisual materials at the point of an instructional problem, for example, a concept derived from the military experience of World War II—were developed and known in a few audiovisual circles. A certain amount of incentive and public acceptance, also derived from World War II experience, could be drawn upon. The cake of custom, however, proved to be too tough. The mass production stage, at least 100 years behind industry, was not entered except here and there on isolated little islands.

It was at this point, approximately in 1955, that the god came out of the machine in the form of the Ford Foundation. Dr. Alvin C. Eurich (and a little later, his associate, Dr. Alexander J. Stoddard) gave the instructional processes of American education a sharp push into mass production technology. The time was ripe. There was a shortage of teachers; education and educationists were under fire from all sides; Neo-Technocracy was turning its attention to education; the race with Russia was underway; the natives were restless indeed.

There are several interesting facets to this shove into mass instructional technology. First, television, both closed-circuit and broadcast, was chosen as the prime hardware. This was due, I think, to the unconsciously assumed basic concept of *mass production*, usually stated in terms of a shortage of teachers, large classes, and quality instruction. Second, the Ford impetus made provision, for the first time, for a technology of systems to go along with the hardware. Stoddard's own work in designing the school of tomorrow (1957) and the work of Trump and his associates in drawing the instructional images of the future for the American secondary school (1959) are, essentially, proposed systems.

Third, the Ford group made use of technology in creating the impetus in the first place. The technology of social psychology and public relations was drawn upon; educational decision-makers were the prime targets, and the means used, including high-priced public relations counsel, were the best available. This accounts for the fact that the teaching profession in general and audiovisual specialists in particular—the latter are really the only technologists of the profession—were for the most part left out of this move into technology.

Instead, the Foundation went to administrators and board members and influential opinion makers of all types. Organizations were approached or created: the National Educational Television and Radio Center (now, I believe, under the administration of the Learning Resources Institute), the revitalized National Association of Educational Broadcasters, the Educational Facilities Laboratories, Inc., and others. As a sign of this policy to short-circuit the profession, it is significant that, except for a small grant to promote a seminar or two, the Department of Audiovisual Instruction of the National Education Association was left out of the largesse.

The Ford people assumed, I think, that if the cake of custom was to be broken the priesthood was not the agency to break it. This may mean, in part and as far as audiovisual and curriculum people are concerned, that to an outsider their technological orientation is at the level of the water wheel and the handloom, not the computer and the rocket. It is something to think about. On the other hand, it may also mean in part that the Ford Foundation is merely another instrument of Neo-Technocracy and that these actions forecast even more loss of control of education by the existing pre-technological profession.

IMPACT OF PRESENT TRENDS

With this background of development painted in, we can now come to grips with the impact of the present technology. If we consider education as a societal universe, what happens when we introduce energy into that universe suddenly and on a large scale? That is apparently what is happening.

Two general effects can be predicted by basing our thinking on two analogous concepts. If the concept of entropy holds good in this connection, *the educational system will become more highly organized and less random in nature* (negative entropy will increase); if the laws of social change first stated by William G. Sumner and William F. Ogburn apply, the introduction of a system of technology into the culture will cause *distortions, stresses, and non-predictable effects to increase until a crisis is reached and the culture becomes much different.* Two historical events serve as examples, one taken from Mumford (1955) (the introduction of the clock to regulate the habits of Monks) and one from Muller (the invention of writing in Egypt for the purpose of keeping accounts) (1959). Both changed the world several times over. The effects of neither were, of course, predictable.

What, then, are the present trends? If you don't count the continuous, grinding, sweating struggle carried on by audiovisual specialists, dealers, manufacturers, and producers to introduce, one item at a time, film libraries, projectors, recorders, etc., into the educational system in the slow process of conversion from a pre-industrial technology, two major trends can be identified. These two trends, at the moment, lead in opposite directions.

The first is the trend toward a mass instructional technology and is governed by machines and systems suitable for that purpose. Foremost, of course, is television, of which there are four instructional types: (1) broadcast on an educational channel, (2) broadcast on a commercial channel, (3) closed-circuit of the Hagerstown-Penn State type in which live instructors are used either to supplement instruction or to provide direct instruction exclusive of classroom teachers, and (4) the Compton type in which filmed lectures are distributed via the closed-circuit medium as replacement for classroom teachers. In all cases, the desire is to reach more students with fewer teachers or to obtain "quality" instruction.

Mass instruction technology in another form includes, of course, the massed film systems. The prime example is the EBF series in physics and chemistry, amounting to over 300 half-hour motion pictures intended to be used where there are no science teachers, where there are teachers not considered qualified, as audiovisual aids to more qualified teachers, and with very large groups of students. These films, of course, may theoretically be used over television. The exploitation of the overhead transparency projector is another example of mass instructional technology as shown in the Newton, Massachusetts experiment in English and grammar and composition.

In opposition to this trend of mass instruction is a growing technology for individual instruction. This trend is the audiovisual wave of the future (for the moment). The most dramatic development here is that class of systems and instruments known as teaching machines. Actually, I would class all teaching equipment designed for individual or near-individual operation as being in the category of teaching machines.[3] At present, then, there are approximately five types, listed here on an ascending scale of sophistication: (1) individual reading papers and similar devices, (2) individual viewing and listening equipment for existing slides, filmstrips, motion pictures, and recordings, (3) language laboratories of all types, (4) specifically programmed printed materials such as scrambled textbooks and the Lumsdaine notebook, and (5) true teaching machines of the Skinner or Pressey type containing carefully worked out verbal or pictorial programs with various ingenious mechanical or electronic arrangements to test student reaction and inform him of his progress, errors, etc.

EXTRAPOLATION I

These two major trends toward technologies of mass and of individual instruction are not science fiction; they are with us now. Assessment of this impact is our most pressing and difficult problem. It does not take much of a crystal ball to see that a combination of these two technologies is the next immediate step. For example, let us take Maurice Mitchell's new series for his chemistry course on 150 plus films. Let us further assume that Mr.

---

[3] Preferred terms in some quarters are "self-instructional" and "auto-instructional" devices.

Mitchell makes a deal with the Rheem Califone Corporation to program their teaching machine with material to go along with the chemistry films. (Mr. Eurich might have to put up the money for the initial effort.) Let us continue by saying we will project the films hourly on the Compton College closed-circut television film distribution system and place the machines in proper cubbyholes for Compton College students to work at specified times. We could get, almost immediately, to what can be called *total educational automation.*

Or, in another context, let us suppose that the new Ford creation, the Learning Resources Institute, initiates another Continental Classroom in mathematics over national broadcast television; and that the new audiovisual teaching machines now being developed are programmed to relate to this new series; and that these machines are placed by the foundation in every public library in America; and that, at the conclusion of the instructional period, students report to designated centers where the Educational Testing Service examines them and certifies them to the colleges of their choice. Think, for a moment, about that one. It is now possible not only to eliminate the teachers but the school system.[4]

These may be considered extreme applications, but such applications, at least experimentally, are inevitable. In fact, one such study, testing the combination of these two technologies, is now underway. The point is that both the mass instruction systems and the technology of individual instruction—teaching machines—are getting terrific momentum. These technologies are going to hit education with a million-pound thrust. What will be the effect upon our educational society? What is the role of the teacher, the audiovisual specialist, the curriculum director? *Quo vadis* the curriculum itself? This last question is particularly pertinent if the medium or image governs the message, as McLuhan maintains.

[4] *Time* magazine had some fun lifting this sentence out of context. See *Time*, March 14, 1959, p. 68. *Time* also said: "Finn offered one caveat: this awesome equipment must not fall into the hands of any one private institution, e.g., the Ford Foundation. Said he, 'The American people don't elect representatives to the Ford Foundation.'"

EXTRAPOLATION II

Technology never sits still. The extrapolations given in the last section are immediate. What of those that can be made for a time slightly farther into the future? I see several developments. First, it is reasonable to expect that programming for teaching machines will move from the verbal-Socratic-Skinner type to the audiovisual-branching type. That is, the machines will present conceptual content based upon student pretests, using films, slides, filmstrips, tapes, and/or videotape as the medium. The presentation sequences will be longer and the student will be given an opportunity to select additional sequences for further explanation if the machine, through testing, informs him that he needs it. Records, of course, will be maintained instantaneously by miniaturized computers.

Secondly, the work in England of Ashby, Pask, and others with teaching machines based on the design concepts of biological computers will affect the technology of the present teaching machines much as transactional psychology affects stimulus-response psychology. Pask has already produced a machine which, in training key punch operators, actually senses the characteristics of the student as he works and automatically adjusts the program of the machine to the student's individual needs. This is a pure transaction, and Pask maintains he can develop such a machine to teach decision-making with present hardware and know-how (1958).

A second development of the future begins next fall with the Airborne TV experiment of the Ford Foundation over a city in Indiana. Circling overhead one or more airplanes carrying multiple television transmitters can broadcast signals over much greater distance than conventional tower transmission. The programs will go into several states and, because of the location, into both urban and rural areas and into innumerable heretofore independent school districts. Effects of this on local control of curricula, curriculum planning procedures, images of master teachers, patterns of school organization, etc., have yet to be speculated about, let alone explored. Nothing technical would prevent, by the way, a national network of such aircraft as an addition to our other national means of transmission.

A third predicted development is based on information that it is technically possible, although not yet economically feasible, to produce a motion picture film with characteristics similar to the Polaroid film that is instantaneously developable. What this would do to videotape, to production techniques, and to the possibilities of local production of materials is of great interest to the audiovisual field.[5]

TEACHER CONTROL

The fourth development that can be anticipated is the most spectacular. Essentially, it is based on a systems concept. It is theoretically possible now to design an automatic classroom under the control of the teacher. Most of the elements are present or can be designed. Such a classroom would have total light and air control, automatic projection and television systems, technical provision for the best possible dicussion environment, display situations, etc., which could be changed at will. By planned programming, the classroom could be made to function for major presentations, small group discussions, individual work at teaching machines, creative periods, and the like. As we said, all of this *could be* under the control of the teacher. The classroom then would become the teaching machine. Adrian TerLouw at Eastman Kodak has done some work in this area and it is, of course, implied in the provocative article by Simon Ramo which is so often cited in discussions of teaching machines (1957). An acquaintance of mine refers to this concept as the "mad scientist" classroom.

IMPLICATIONS

To assess the implications of this current and predicted impact of technology on the instructional process is not easy. As with any such speculation, it is also hazardous. It is, however, a job we must attempt.

[5] The new thermo-plastic method of image-recording developed by General Electric can do much the same thing.

We have to start, I think, with the proposition that our educational society is in the position of a backward or underdeveloped culture suddenly assailed by the 20th-century engineer. In addition, reactions in some professional circles to the advent of television are similar to those factory workers of the 19th century who attempted to destroy the machines that were taking over their jobs. In the long run, the machines remained; instructional technology is, no doubt, here to stay. Our problem becomes one, not so much of how to live with it on some kind of feather-bedding basis as how to control it so that the proper objectives of education may be served and the human being remain central in the process.

Certain things are obvious. I think the concept of negative entropy[6] will hold. The thrust and energy of technology will force a greater organization upon us at every point *at which it is applied to instruction*. Such an arrangement as the Airborne experiment will require a tighter and different organization in those five or six states and in those many school districts of the Midwest. The closed-circuit experiment begun a year ago in Anaheim, California, is already, it seems to me, making requirements for organization—of scope and sequence in the curriculum, of the district itself, and of the nature of the television presentations—the rigor of which has never been felt before in Anaheim.

Programming, in its machine, computer, and automation sense, is a matter of extreme organization—the piling up of energy.[7] Most of the devices and systems of the new technology require, one way or another, this type of programming—television, teaching machines, mass films, language laboratories. This means that programmers are needed. Who is to do this? This is essentially, in the old sense, both a curriculum and an audiovisual problem.

---

[6] In all the tests I have been able to think of, this concept holds. I am almost convinced that this idea can achieve some status as, forgive me, "Finn's law."

[7] The role of energy in relation to AV communication theory needs much study. For example, the energy involved in the negative entropy concept should be examined in much the same way that Cottrell studied energy in general in *Energy and Society*.

It is also a social problem. The heartland is programming. He who controls the programming heartland controls the educational system. Will it be a foundation, a committee of scientists, textbook publishers and film producers, the NEA, the school superintendent, the board of education, the students, or the general public?

Too, how many of us will go overboard and sink with the old concepts that will be absorbed or outmoded and tossed to the sharks by the new technology? Take the concept of instructional materials which some curriculum specialists love so well and which caused quite a controversy in DAVI circles a few years ago. The fight was futile, as is the love. The concept of programming and the systems and systems analysis it implies completely absorbs the idea of materials. Instructional materials becomes an outmoded, atomistic, pre-technological concept useful mainly to the historians of education.[8]

The concept of audiovisual education may accompany instructional materials down the drain, or it may not, depending on whether or not it can be redefined acceptably.[9] The Skinner and Pressey type teaching machines and their descendants are, for example, primarily verbal devices, and yet their management and programming as technical electronic devices belong somewhere. At a practical level, within a school situation, someone is going to have to worry about them. It is my contention that the audiovisual field is in the easiest position to help integrate these mechanisms properly into the instructional process. They are not primarily audiovisual; they are primarily technological. The AV field, I think, must now suddenly grow up. We, the audiovisual specialists, are, of all educational personnel, the closest to technology now; we have, I think, to become specialists in *learning technology*—and that's how I would redefine audiovisual education.

What of the curriculum people? Their work is just beginning. It can become infinitely more rigorous and

[8] McLuhan maintains the same thing about audiovisual aids (1959).
[9] Redefinition (and terminology) of the audiovisual field are contemplated as subject of a future special supplement to AV COMMUNICATION REVIEW.

at the same time more satisfying. I suspect some of the emotional Rousseauians will have to get out of the curriculum business. The rest can step in and face this problem of programming a learning technology in human terms and find great excitement and reward. The profession as a whole must be made to sense this powerful movement to instructional technology and be made ready to seize the great opportunity it offers to make *all* teachers highly professional.

THE PHILOSOPHY OF ADVENTURE

In closing, I should like to quote Whitehead, who said that it is the business of the future to be dangerous. Technology certainly has made this aphorism into the outstanding fact of our time. Technology is now making the future of instruction capricious and hazardous. But in doing so it has presented us with more opportunity and more choices than ever before. If the future is an adventure, it is an adventure *because* of technology. The cost of civilization is the fact that we can make wrong choices because of the alternatives technology presents. The reward of civilization is the freedom provided by technology and the opportunity to make the right choices. This cost and this reward we now face with the technology of the instructional process. We *must* look forward to the adventure and not present what Herbert Muller noted as "the curious spectacle of civilized man forever marching with his face turned backward—as no doubt the cave man looked back to the good old days when men were free to roam instead of being stuck in a damn hole in the ground" (p. 65). The "good old days" are gone; approached with intelligence and zest, the days of the future will be better.

REFERENCES

McLUHAN, MARSHALL, What fundamental changes are foreshadowed in the prevailing patterns of educational organization and methods of instruction by the revolution in electronics? *Current Issues in Higher Education*, 1959. Washington, D.C.: Association for Higher Education, NEA, 176-182.

MULLER, HERBERT. *The Uses of the Past.* New York: Oxford Univ. 1959, p. 48.

MUMFORD, LEWIS. *The Human Prospect.* Boston: Beacon, 1955, 3-9.

OLIVER, J. W. *The History of American Technology.* New York: Ronald, 1956, 298-299.

PASK, GORDON, Electronic keyboard teaching machines, *Education and Commerce*, 1958, **24**, 16-26.

RAMO, SIMON, A new technique of education, *Engineering and Science*, 1957, **21**, 17-22.

STODDARD, A. J. *Schools for Tomorrow.* New York: The Fund for the Advancement of Education, 1957.

TRUMP, J. L. *Images of the Future.* Washington, D.C.: National Association of Secondary School Principles, NEA, 1959 (48 p.).

2

The Science of Learning and the Art of Teaching*

B. F. SKINNER
Harvard University

Some promising advances have recently been made in the field of learning. Special techniques have been designed to arrange what are called "contingencies of reinforcement"—the relations which prevail between behavior on the one hand and the consequences of that behavior on the other—with the result that a much more effective control of behavior has been achieved. It has long been argued that an organism learns mainly by producing changes in its environment, but it is only recently that these changes have been carefully manipulated. In traditional devices for the study of learning—in the serial maze, for example, or in the T-maze, the problem box, or the familiar discrimination apparatus—the effects produced by the organism's behavior are left to many fluctuating circumstances. There is many a slip between the turn-to-the-right and the food-cup at the end of the alley. It is not surprising that techniques of this sort have yielded only very rough data from which the uniformities demanded by an experimental science can be

---

* Paper presented at a conference on Current Trends in Psychology and the Behavioral Sciences at the University of Pittsburgh, March 12, 1954. This article is reprinted from the *Harvard Educational Review*, 1954, 24, 86-97, and is used here with the permission of the author and the editors.

extracted only by averaging many cases. In none of this work has the behavior of the individual organism been predicted in more than a statistical sense. The learning processes which are the presumed object of such research are reached only through a series of inferences. Current preoccupation with deductive systems reflects this state of the science.

Recent improvements in the conditions which control behavior in the field of learning are of two principal sorts. The Law of Effect has been taken seriously; we have made sure that effects *do* occur and that they occur under conditions which are optimal for producing the changes called learning. Once we have arranged the particular type of consequence called a reinforcement, our techniques permit us to shape up the behavior of an organism almost at will. It has become a routine exercise to demonstrate this in classes in elementary psychology by conditioning such an organism as a pigeon. Simply by presenting food to a hungry pigeon at the right time, it is possible to shape up three or four well-defined responses in a single demonstration period—such responses as turning around, pacing the floor in the pattern of a figure-8, standing still in a corner of the demonstration apparatus, stretching the neck, or stamping the foot. Extremely complex performances may be reached through successive stages in the shaping process, the contingencies of reinforcement being changed progressively in the direction of the required behavior. The results are often quite dramatic. In such a demonstration one can *see* learning take place. A significant change in behavior is often obvious as the result of a single reinforcement.

A second important advance in technique permits us to maintain behavior in given states of strength for long periods of time. Reinforcements continue to be important, of course, long after an organism has learned *how* to do something, long after it has acquired behavior. They are necessary to maintain the behavior in strength. Of special interest is the effect of various schedules of intermittent reinforcement. Charles B. Ferster and the author are currently preparing an extensive report of a five-year research program, sponsored by the Office of Naval Research, in which most of the important types of schedules have been investigated and in which the effects of schedules in general have been reduced to a few principles. On the theoretical side we now have a fairly good idea of why a given schedule produces its appropriate performance. On the practical side we have learned how to maintain any given level of activity for daily periods limited only by the physical exhaustion of the organism and from day to day without substantial change throughout its life. Many of these effects would be traditionally assigned to the field of motivation, although the principal operation is simply the arrangement of contingencies of reinforcement.[1]

These new methods of shaping behavior and of maintaining it in strength are a great improvement over the traditional practices of professional animal trainers, and it is not surprising that our laboratory results are already being applied to the production of performing animals for commercial purposes. In a more academic environment they have been used for demonstration purposes which extend far beyond an interest in learning as such. For example, it is not too difficult to arrange the complex contingencies which produce many types of social behavior. Competition is exemplified by two pigeons playing a modified game of ping-pong. The pigeons drive the ball back and forth across a small table by pecking at it. When the ball gets by one pigeon, the other is reinforced. The task of constructing such a "social relation" is probably completely out of reach of the traditional animal trainer. It requires a carefully designed program of gradually changing contingencies and the skillful use of schedules to maintain the behavior in strength. Each pigeon is separately prepared for its part in the total performance, and the "social relation" is then arbitrarily constructed. The sequence of events leading up to this stable state are excellent material for the study of the factors important in nonsynthetic social behavior. It is instructive to consider how a similar series of contin-

---

[1] The reader may wish to review Dr. Skinner's article, "Some Contributions of an Experimental Analysis of Behavior to Psychology as a Whole," *The American Psychologist*, 1953, **8**, 69-78. Ed.

gencies could arise in the case of the human organism through the evolution of cultural patterns.

Cooperation can also be set up, perhaps more easily than competition. We have trained two pigeons to coordinate their behavior in a cooperative endeavor with a precision which equals that of the most skillful human dancers. In a more serious vein these techniques have permitted us to explore the complexities of the individual organism and to analyze some of the serial or coordinate behaviors involved in attention, problem solving, various types of self-control, and the subsidiary systems of responses within a single organism called "personalities." Some of these are exemplified in what we call multiple schedules of reinforcement. In general a given schedule has an effect upon the rate at which a response is emitted. Changes in the rate from moment to moment show a pattern typical of the schedule. The pattern may be as simple as a constant rate of responding at a given value, it may be a gradually accelerating rate between certain extremes, it may be an abrupt change from not responding at all to a given stable high rate, and so on. It has been shown that the performance characteristic of a given schedule can be brought under the control of a particular stimulus and that different performances can be brought under the control of different stimuli in the same organism. At a recent meeting of the American Psychological Association, Dr. Ferster and the author demonstrated a pigeon whose behavior showed the pattern typical of "fixed-interval" reinforcement in the presence of one stimulus and, alternately, the pattern typical of the very different schedule called "fixed ratio" in the presence of a second stimulus. In the laboratory we have been able to obtain performances appropriate to *nine* different schedules in the presence of appropriate stimuli in random alternation. When Stimulus 1 is present, the pigeon executes the performance appropriate to Schedule 1. When Stimulus 2 is present, the pigeon executes the performance appropriate to Schedule 2. And so on. This result is important because it makes the extrapolation of our laboratory results to daily life much more plausible. We are all constantly shifting from schedule to schedule as our immediate environment changes, but the dynamics of the control exercised by reinforcement remain essentially unchanged.

It is also possible to construct very complex *sequences* of schedules. It is not easy to describe these in a few words, but two or three examples may be mentioned. In one experiment the pigeon generates a performance appropriate to Schedule A where the reinforcement is simply the production of the stimulus characteristic of Schedule B, to which the pigeon then responds appropriately. Under a third stimulus, the bird yields a performance appropriate to Schedule C where the reinforcement in this case is simply the production of the stimulus characteristic of Schedule D, to which the bird then responds appropriately. In a special case, first investigated by L. B. Wyckoff, Jr., the organism responds to one stimulus where the reinforcement consists of the *clarification* of the stimulus controlling another response. The first response becomes, so to speak, an objective form of "paying attention" to the second stimulus. In one important version of this experiment, as yet unpublished, we could say that the pigeon is telling us whether it is "paying attention" to the *shape* of a spot of light or to its *color*.

One of the most dramatic applications of these techniques has recently been made in the Harvard Psychological Laboratories by Floyd Ratliff and Donald S. Blough, who have skillfully used multiple and serial schedules of reinforcement to study complex perceptual processes in the infrahuman organism. They have achieved a sort of psycho-physics without verbal instruction. In a recent experiment by Blough, for example, a pigeon draws a detailed dark-adaptation curve showing the characteristic breaks of rod and cone vision. The curve is recorded continuously in a single experimental period and is quite comparable with the curves of human subjects. The pigeon behaves in a way which, in the human case, we would not hesitate to describe by saying that it adjusts a very faint patch of light until it can just be seen.

In all this work, the species of the organism has made surprisingly little difference. It is true that the organisms studied have all been vertebrates, but they still cover a wide range. Comparable results have been obtained with pigeons, rats, dogs, monkeys, human children, and most recently, by the author in collaboration with Ogden R. Lindsley, human psychotic subjects. In spite of great phylogenetic differences, all these organisms show amazingly similar properties of the learning process. It should be emphasized that this has been achieved by analyzing the effects of reinforcement and by designing techniques which manipulate reinforcement with considerable precision. Only in this way can the behavior of the individual organism be brought under such precise control. It is also important to note that through a gradual advance to complex interrelations among responses, the same degree of rigor is being extended to behavior which would usually be assigned to such fields as perception, thinking, and personality dynamics.

From this exciting prospect of an advancing science of learning, it is a great shock to turn to that branch of technology which is most directly concerned with the learning process—education. Let us consider, for example, the teaching of arithmetic in the lower grades. The school is concerned with imparting to the child a large number of responses of a special sort. The responses are all verbal. They consist of speaking and writing certain words, figures, and signs which, to put it roughly, refer to numbers and to arithmetic operations. The first task is to shape up these responses—to get the child to pronounce and to write responses correctly, but the principal task is to bring this behavior under many sorts of stimulus control. This is what happens when the child learns to count, to recite tables, to count while ticking off the items in an assemblage of objects, to respond to spoken or written numbers by saying "odd," "even," "prime," and so on. Over and above this elaborate repertoire of numerical behavior, most of which is often dismissed as the product of rote learning, the teaching of arithmetic looks forward to those complex serial arrangements of responses involved in original mathematical thinking. The child must acquire responses of transposing, clearing fractions, and so on, which modify the order or pattern of the original material so that the response called a solution is eventually made possible.

Now, how is this extremely complicated verbal repertoire set up? In the first place, what reinforcements are used? Fifty years ago the answer would have been clear. At that time educational control was still frankly aversive. The child read numbers, copied numbers, memorized tables, and performed operations upon numbers to escape the threat of the birch rod or cane. Some positive reinforcements were perhaps eventually derived from the increased efficiency of the child in the field of arithmetic and in rare cases some automatic reinforcement may have resulted from the sheer manipulation of the medium—from the solution of problems or the discovery of the intricacies of the number system. But for the immediate purposes of education the child acted to avoid or escape punishment. It was part of the reform movement known as progressive education to make the positive consequences more immediately effective, but any one who visits the lower grades of the average school today will observe that a change has been made, not from aversive to positive control, but from one form of aversive stimulation to another. The child at his desk, filling in his workbook, is behaving primarily to escape from the threat of a series of minor aversive events—the teacher's displeasure, the criticism or ridicule of his classmates, an ignominious showing in a competition, low marks, a trip to the office "to be talked to" by the principal, or a word to the parent who may still resort to the birch rod. In this welter of aversive consequences, getting the right answer is in itself an insignificant event, any effect of which is lost amid the anxieties, the boredom, and the aggressions which are the inevitable by-products of aversive control.[2]

Secondly, we have to ask how the contingencies of reinforcement are arranged. When is a numerical operation reinforced as "right"? Eventually, of course, the pupil may be able to check his own answers and achieve some sort of automatic reinforcement, but in the early stages the reinforcement of being right is usually accorded by the teacher. The contingencies she provides are far from optimal. It can easily be demonstrated that, unless explicit mediating behavior has been set up, the lapse of

[2] SKINNER, B. F. *Science and Human Behavior.* New York: Macmillan, 1953.

only a few seconds between response and reinforcement destroys most of the effect. In a typical classroom, nevertheless, long periods of time customarily elapse. The teacher may walk up and down the aisle, for example, while the class is working on a sheet of problems, pausing here and there to say right or wrong. Many seconds or minutes intervene between the child's response and the teacher's reinforcement. In many cases—for example, when papers are taken home to be corrected—as much as 24 hours may intervene. It is surprising that this system has any effect whatsoever.

A third notable shortcoming is the lack of a skillful program which moves forward through a series of progressive approximations to the final complex behavior desired. A long series of contingencies is necessary to bring the organism into the possession of mathematical behavior most efficiently. But the teacher is seldom able to reinforce at each step in such a series because she cannot deal with the pupil's responses one at a time. It is usually necessary to reinforce the behavior in blocks of responses—as in correcting a work sheet or page from a workbook. The responses within such a block must not be interrelated. The answer to one problem must not depend upon the answer to another. The number of stages through which one may progressively approach a complex pattern of behavior is therefore small, and the task so much the more difficult. Even the most modern workbook in beginning arithmetic is far from exemplifying an efficient program for shaping up mathematical behavior.

Perhaps the most serious criticism of the current classroom is the relative infrequency of reinforcement. Since the pupil is usually dependent upon the teacher for being right, and since many pupils are usually dependent upon the same teacher, the total number of contingencies which may be arranged during, say, the first four years, is of the order of only a few thousand. But a very rough estimate suggests that efficient mathematical behavior at this level requires something of the order of 25,000 contingencies. We may suppose that even in the brighter student a given contingency must be arranged several times to place the behavior well in hand. The responses to be set up are not simply the various items in tables of addition, subtraction, multiplication, and division; we have also to consider the alternative forms in which each item may be stated. To the learning of such material we should add hundreds of responses concerned with factoring, identifying primes, memorizing series, using short-cut techniques of calculation, constructing and using geometric representations or number forms, and so on. Over and above all this, the whole mathematical repertoire must be brought under the control of concrete problems of considerable variety. Perhaps 50,000 contingencies is a more conservative estimate. In this frame of reference the daily assignment in arithmetic seems pitifully meagre.

The result of all this is, of course, well known. Even our best schools are under criticism for their inefficiency in the teaching of drill subjects such as arithmetic. The condition in the average school is a matter of widespread national concern. Modern children simply do not learn arithmetic quickly or well. Nor is the result simply incompetence. The very subjects in which modern techniques are weakest are those in which failure is most conspicuous, and in the wake of an ever-growing incompetence come the anxieties, uncertainties, and aggressions which in their turn present other problems to the school. Most pupils soon claim the asylum of not being "ready" for arithmetic at a given level or, eventually, of not having a mathematical mind. Such explanations are readily seized upon by defensive teachers and parents. Few pupils ever reach the stage at which automatic reinforcements follow as the natural consequences of mathematical behavior. On the contrary, the figures and symbols of mathematics have become standard emotional stimuli. The glimpse of a column of figures, not to say an algebraic symbol or an integral sign, is likely to set off—not mathematical behavior—but a reaction of anxiety, guilt, or fear.

The teacher is usually no happier about this than the pupil. Denied the opportunity to control via the birch rod, quite at sea as to the mode of operation of the few techniques at her disposal, she spends as little time as possible on drill subjects and eagerly subscribes to philosophies of education which emphasize material of greater inherent interest. A confession of weakness is her extraordinary concern lest the child be taught something unnecessary. The repertoire to be imparted is carefully reduced to an essential minimum. In the field of spelling, for example, a great deal of time and energy has gone into discovering just those words which the young child is going to use, as if it were a crime to waste one's educational power in teaching an unnecessary word. Eventually, weakness of technique emerges in the disguise of a reformulation of the aims of education. Skills are minimized in favor of vague achievements—educating for democracy, educating the whole child, educating for life, and so on. And there the matter ends; for, unfortunately, these philosophies do not in turn suggest improvements in techniques. They offer little or no help in the design of better classroom practices.

There would be no point in urging these objections if improvement were impossible. But the advances which have recently been made in our control of the learning process suggest a thorough revision of classroom practices and, fortunately, they tell us how the revision can be brought about. This is not, of course, the first time that the results of an experimental science have been brought to bear upon the practical problems of education. The modern classroom does not, however, offer much evidence that research in the field of learning has been respected or used. This condition is no doubt partly due to the limitations of earlier research. But it has been encouraged by a too hasty conclusion that the laboratory study of learning is inherently limited because it cannot take into account the realities of the classroom. In the light of our increasing knowledge of the learning process we should, instead, insist upon dealing with those realities and forcing a substantial change in them. Education is perhaps the most important branch of scientific technology. It deeply affects the lives of all of us. We can no longer allow the exigencies of a practical situation to suppress the tremendous improvements which are within reach. The practical situation must be changed.

There are certain questions which have to be answered in turning to the study of any new organism. What behavior is to be set up? What reinforcers are at hand? What responses are available in embarking upon a program of progressive approximation which will lead to the final form of the behavior? How can reinforcements be most efficiently scheduled to maintain the behavior in strength? These questions are all relevant in considering the problem of the child in the lower grades.

In the first place, what reinforcements are available? What does the school have in its possession which will reinforce a child? We may look first to the material to be learned, for it is possible that this will provide considerable automatic reinforcement. Children play for hours with mechanical toys, paints, scissors and paper, noise-makers, puzzles—in short, with almost anything which feeds back significant changes in the environment and is reasonably free of aversive properties. The sheer control of nature is itself reinforcing. This effect is not evident in the modern school because it is masked by the emotional responses generated by aversive control. It is true that automatic reinforcement from the manipulation of the environment is probably only a mild reinforcer and may need to be carefully husbanded, but one of the most striking principles to emerge from recent research is that the *net* amount of reinforcement is of little significance. A very slight reinforcement may be tremendously effective in controlling behavior if it is wisely used.

If the natural reinforcement inherent in the subject matter is not enough, other reinforcers must be employed. Even in school the child is occasionally permitted to do "what he wants to do," and access to reinforcements of many sorts may be made contingent upon the more immediate consequences of the behavior to be established. Those who advocate competition as a useful social motive may wish to use the reinforcements which follow from excelling others, although there is the difficulty that in this case the reinforcement of one child is necessarily aversive to another. Next in order we might place the good will and affection of the teacher, and only when that has failed need we turn to the use of aversive stimulation.

In the second place, how are these reinforcements to be made contingent upon the desired behavior? There are two considerations here—the gradual elaboration of extremely complex patterns of behavior and the maintenance of the behavior in strength at each stage. The whole process of becoming competent in any field must be divided into a very large number of very small steps, and reinforcement must be contingent upon the accomplishment of each step. This solution to the problem of creating a complex repertoire of behavior also solves the problem of maintaining the behavior in strength. We could, of course, resort to the techniques of scheduling already developed in the study of other organisms but in the present state of our knowledge of educational practices, scheduling appears to be most effectively arranged through the design of the material to be learned. By making each successive step as small as possible, the frequency of reinforcement can be raised to a maximum, while the possibly aversive consequences of being wrong are reduced to a minimum. Other ways of designing material would yield other programs of reinforcement. Any supplementary reinforcement would probably have to be scheduled in the more traditional way.

These requirements are not excessive, but they are probably incompatible with the current realities of the classroom. In the experimental study of learning it has been found that the contingencies of reinforcement which are most efficient in controlling the organism cannot be arranged through the personal mediation of the experimenter. An organism is affected by subtle details of contingencies which are beyond the capacity of the human organism to arrange. Mechanical and electrical devices must be used. Mechanical help is also demanded by the sheer number of contingencies which may be used efficiently in a single experimental session. We have recorded many millions of responses from a single organism during thousands of experimental hours. Personal arrangement of the contingencies and personal observation of the results are quite unthinkable. Now, the human organism is, if anything, more sensitive to precise contingencies than the other organisms we have studied. We have every reason to expect, therefore, that the most effective control of human learning will require instrumental aid. The simple fact is that, as a mere re-

inforcing mechanism, the teacher is out of date. This
would be true even if a single teacher devoted all her
time to a single child, but her inadequacy is multiplied
many-fold when she must serve as a reinforcing device to
many children at once. If the teacher is to take advantage
of recent advances in the study of learning, she must have
the help of mechanical devices.

The technical problem of providing the necessary instrumental aid is not particularly difficult. There are
many ways in which the necessary contingencies may be
arranged, either mechanically or electrically. An inexpen-
sive device which solves most of the principal problems
has already been constructed. It is still in the experimental stage, but a description will suggest the kind of instrument which seems to be required. The device consists of a small box about the size of a small record player.
On the top surface is a window through which a question
or problem printed on a paper tape may be seen. The
child answers the question by moving one or more sliders
upon which the digits 0 through 9 are printed. The answer appears in square holes punched in the paper upon
which the question is printed. When the answer has been
set, the child turns a knob. The operation is as simple as
adjusting a television set. If the answer is right, the knob
turns freely and can be made to ring a bell or provide
some other conditioned reinforcement. If the answer is
wrong, the knob will not turn. A counter may be added
to tally wrong answers. The knob must then be reversed
slightly and a second attempt at a right answer made.
(Unlike the flash-card, the device reports a wrong answer without giving the right answer.) When the answer
is right, a further turn of the knob engages a clutch
which moves the next problem into place in the window.
This movement cannot be completed, however, until the
sliders have been returned to zero.

The important features of the device are these: Reinforcement for the right answer is immediate. The mere
manipulation of the device will probably be reinforcing
enough to keep the average pupil at work for a suitable
period each day, provided traces of earlier aversive control can be wiped out. A teacher may supervise an entire
class at work on such devices at the same time, yet each

child may progress at his own rate, completing as many problems as possible within the class period. If forced to be away from school, he may return to pick up where he left off. The gifted child will advance rapidly, but can be kept from getting too far ahead either by being excused from arithmetic for a time or by being given special sets of problems which take him into some of the interesting bypaths of mathematics.

The device makes it possible to present carefully designed material in which one problem can depend upon the answer to the preceding and where, therefore, the most efficient progress to an eventually complex repertoire can be made. Provision has been made for recording the commonest mistakes so that the tapes can be modified as experience dictates. Additional steps can be inserted where pupils tend to have trouble, and ultimately the material will reach a point at which the answers of the average child will almost always be right.

If the material itself proves not to be sufficiently reinforcing, other reinforcers in the possession of the teacher or school may be made contingent upon the operation of the device or upon progress through a series of problems. Supplemental reinforcement would not sacrifice the advantages gained from immediate reinforcement and from the possibility of constructing an optimal series of steps which approach the complex repertoire of mathematical behavior most efficiently.

A similar device in which the sliders carry the letters of the alphabet has been designed to teach spelling. In addition to the advantages which can be gained from precise reinforcement and careful programming, the device will teach reading at the same time. It can also be used to establish the large and important repertoire of verbal relationships encountered in logic and science. In short, it can teach verbal thinking. As to content instruction, the device can be operated as a multiple-choice self-rater.

Some objections to the use of such devices in the classroom can easily be foreseen. The cry will be raised that the child is being treated as a mere animal and that an essentially human intellectual achievement is being analyzed in unduly mechanistic terms. Mathematical behavior is usually regarded, not as a repertoire of re-

SCIENCE OF LEARNING AND ART OF TEACHING

as evidences of mathematical ability or the exercise of the
power of reason. It is true that the techniques which
are emerging from the experimental study of learning are
not designed to "develop the mind" or to further some
vague "understanding" of mathematical relationships.
They are designed, on the contrary, to establish the very
behaviors which are taken to be the evidences of such
mental states or processes. This is only a special case of
the general change which is under way in the interpretation of human affairs. An advancing science continues to
offer more and more convincing alternatives to traditional
formulations. The behavior in terms of which human
thinking must eventually be defined is worth treating in
its own right as the substantial goal of education.

Of course the teacher has a more important function
than to say right or wrong. The changes proposed would
free her for the effective exercise of that function. Mark-
ing a set of papers in arithmetic—"Yes, nine and six *are*
fifteen; no, nine and seven *are not* eighteen"—is beneath
the dignity of any intelligent individual. There is more
important work to be done—in which the teacher's relations to the pupil cannot be duplicated by a mechanical
device. Instrumental help would merely improve these
relations. One might say that the main trouble with
education in the lower grades today is that the child is
obviously not competent and *knows it* and that the
teacher is unable to do anything about it and *knows that
too*. If the advances which have recently been made in
our control of behavior can give the child a genuine competence in reading, writing, spelling, and arithmetic,
then the teacher may begin to function, not in lieu of a
cheap machine, but through intellectual, cultural, and
emotional contacts of that distinctive sort which testify
to her status as a human being.

Another possible objection is that mechanized instruction will mean technological unemployment. We need
not worry about this until there are enough teachers to
go around and until the hours and energy demanded of
the teacher are comparable to those in other fields of
employment. Mechanical devices will eliminate the more
tiresome labors of the teacher but they will not neces-

sarily shorten the time during which she remains in contact with the pupil.

A more practical objection: Can we afford to mechanize our schools? The answer is clearly yes. The device I have just described could be produced as cheaply as a small radio or phonograph. There would need to be far fewer devices than pupils, for they could be used in rotation. But even if we suppose that the instrument eventually found to be most effective would cost several hundred dollars and that large numbers of them would be required, our economy should be able to stand the strain. Once we have accepted the possibility and the necessity of mechanical help in the classroom, the economic problem can easily be surmounted. There is no reason why the school room should be any less mechanized than, for example, the kitchen. A country which annually produces millions of refrigerators, dish-washers, automatic washing-machines, automatic clothes-driers, and automatic garbage disposers can certainly afford the equipment necessary to educate its citizens to high standards of competence in the most effective way.

There is a simple job to be done. The task can be stated in concrete terms. The necessary techniques are known. The equipment needed can easily be provided. Nothing stands in the way but cultural inertia. But what is more characteristic of America than an unwillingness to accept the traditional as inevitable? We are on the threshold of an exciting and revolutionary period, in which the scientific study of man will be put to work in man's best interests. Education must play its part. It must accept the fact that a sweeping revision of educational practices is possible and inevitable. When it has done this, we may look forward with confidence to a school system which is aware of the nature of its tasks, secure in its methods, and generously supported by the informed and effective citizens whom education itself will create.

3

Teaching Machines: An Application of Principles From the Laboratory*

JAMES G. HOLLAND
Harvard University

Much has been said of teaching machines recently—but the emphasis has tended to be on the gadgets rather than on the much more significant development of a new technology of education initiated by B. F. Skinner (1954). The technology does use a device called a teaching machine which presents a finely graded series of problems and provides immediate "reward" or reinforcement for the student's correct answers. But emphasis on machines has tended to obscure the more important facets of the new technology based on application of principles from the laboratory. The machines of today are not necessarily better than those of yesterday. Indeed, adequate machines could have been built hundreds of years ago. The movement today is not simply the mechanization of teaching, but instead the development of a new technology—a behavioral engineering of teaching procedures.

The history of unsuccessful teaching machines illus-

* The work discussed in this paper has been supported by grants from the Carnegie Corporation and the Ford Foundation. This article appeared originally in the *Proceedings* of the 1959 Conference on Testing Problems, Princeton: Educational Testing Service, 1959, and is used here with the permission of the author and the Educational Testing Service.

trates the relatively greater importance of the technique as opposed to the gadgets. The first teaching machine was patented 93 years ago. There have since been a series of patents and a promising burst of activity by Sidney Pressey and his associates (1926). None of these early efforts really caught hold. But during this period in which the idea of mechanized teaching has been latent the science of behavior has developed principles which permit extremely precise control of behavior. This new technology is not only the so-called automation of teaching but is an attempt to obtain the kind of behavioral control shown possible in the laboratory.

We have, of course, seen other practical applications of scientific psychology. We are all familiar with the development of a technology of testing which permits placing an individual in situations suited to his abilities. We are also familiar with another technology called human engineering, which fits machines and jobs to the capacities of man. One places a man in a job that suits him; the other alters the job to suit the man; *neither* attempts to alter or control man's behavior.

For years in the laboratory we *have* controlled the behavior of experimental subjects—both animal and human—by a widening array of principles and techniques. The new technology of education is the application of behavioral laws in modifying or controlling behavior. Such a technology became possible with the realization that we are actually referring to a verbal repertoire (Skinner, 1957) controlled by the same laws as other behavior. The old, defunct explanatory concepts of knowledge, meaning, mind or symbolic processes have never offered the possibility of manipulation or control; but behavior, verbal or otherwise, can be controlled with ease and precision.

While machines are not the essential or defining aspects of this technology, they do play an important role in providing some of this fine control the technology requires. We will now examine several machines and notice the advantages they offer.

At Harvard there is a self-instruction room with ten booths, each containing a machine. The student gets one set of material from the attendant and places it in the machines. He closes the machine and begins his studies.

This machine presents one item of material at a time. The subject reads the statement which has one or more words missing and he completes the statement by writing in the answer space. He then raises the lever and a small shutter opens revealing the correct answer, and simultaneously his answer is moved under glass where it can be read and compared with the new-exposed correct answer. After comparing his answer with the correct answer the student indicates to the machine, with an appropriate movement of the lever, whether his answer was correct or incorrect and the next item appears in the window. All items answered wrong are repeated after he completes the set of items. Correctly answered items are not repeated.

A critical feature of the machine is that it provides immediate reinforcement for correct answers. Being correct is known to be a reinforcer for humans (Perin, 1943). In machine teaching reinforcement is immediate. We know from laboratory work that a delay between a response and its reinforcement of a few seconds will greatly reduce the effectiveness of the reinforcement. Adult humans have developed behavior which serves to mediate small delays; nevertheless, any delay makes reinforcement less effective.

Although other techniques such as programmed workbooks (Homme and Glasser, 1958), "self-correcting" homework (Diederich, 1960), and flash cards are sometimes used in this new behavioral technology, they offer less control. Teaching machines eliminate undesirable forms of responses which would also be successful in obtaining the right answer. For example, the teaching machine insures that the student answer before peeking at the indicated answer. There is a strong temptation to glance ahead with only a poorly formulated, unwritten answer when flashcards are used.

This write-in machine is a prototype of the most common machine. There is another machine used for teaching young children material which consistently has a single possible answer. In the machine the constructed answer is automatically compared with the true answer. The child is presented a problem, perhaps a statement such as $2 + 2 =$ ———, and he must provide the "4." By moving a slider appropriately he can insert the 4 into the answer space. He then turns the crank, and the next item appears immediately, and therefore, immediate reinforcement is provided.

Both of the machines described thus far require the student to compose the answer. A machine for a less mature organism who cannot yet compose an answer can be used for teaching preschool children (Hively, 1960). In this machine there is a large top window and three small windows. In the large window there is some sort of problem, and in the three smaller windows, there are three alternative choices. When the correct choice is made, the next frame is presented.

Enough of machines. They should not be allowed to obscure the truly important feature of the new technology, namely, the application of methods for behavioral control in developing programs for teaching. We need to say no more about the well-known principle of immediate reinforcement. Our second principle is also well known. Behavior is learned only when it is *emitted* and reinforced. But in the classroom, the student performs very little, verbally. However, while working with a machine, the student necessarily emits appropriate behavior and this behavior is usually reinforced since the material is designed so that the student is usually correct. Not only is reinforcement needed for learning, a high density of correct items is necessary because material which generates errors is punishing. Laboratory experiments (Azrin, 1956) have shown that punishment lowers the rate of the punished behavior. In our experience with teaching machines we have also observed that students stop work when the material is so difficult that they make many errors. Furthermore, they become irritated, almost aggressive, when errors are made.

The third important principle is that of gradual progression to establish complex repertoires. A visitor once asked if Skinner had realized that pigeons were so smart before he began using them as subjects. The answer given by a helpful graduate student was that they weren't so smart before Skinner began using them. And indeed they weren't. The behavior developed in many experiments is like that developed in the classroom. Both are complex operants. Both require a careful program of gradual progression. We cannot wait for a student to describe the content of a psychology course and then reinforce the performance; nor can we wait for a pigeon to emit such an improbable bit of behavior as turning a circle, facing a disk on the wall, pecking it if lit, and then bending down to a new exposed food tray and eating.

When developing a complex performance in a pigeon, we may first reinforce simply the behavior of approaching the food tray when it is presented with a loud click. Later the pigeon learns to peck a key which produces the click and the food tray. Still later, he may learn to peck this key only when it is lit, the peck being followed by the loud click and approach to the food tray. In the next step, he may learn to raise his head or hop from one foot to another, or walk a figure eight, in order to produce the lighted key which he then pecks; the click follows; and he approaches the food tray.

This principle of gradual progression runs through many of the teaching machine techniques. Both human and avian scholars deserve the same careful tutorage. The teaching machine program moves in very finely graded steps, working from simple to an ever higher level of complexity. Such a gradual development is illustrated in Table 1 by a few items taken from a psychology program (Holland and Skinner).

The principle of gradual progression serves not simply to make the student correct as often as possible, but it is also the fastest way to develop a complex repertoire. In fact, a new complex operant may never appear except through separately reinforcing members of a graded series (Keller and Schoenfield, 1950). Only this way can we quickly create a *new pattern* of behavior. The pigeon would not have learned the complex sequence necessary to receive the food if he had not learned each step in its proper order. Obviously a child can't begin with advanced mathematics, but neither can he begin with $2 + 2 = 4$—even this is too complex and requires a gradual progression.

Our fourth principle is, in a sense, another form of gradual progression—one which involves the gradual

TABLE 1

Items from the psychology program (Holland and Skinner).
These items illustrate the gradual development of a new concept.

Item	Correct Answer	Percentage of Students Giving the Answer
1. Performing animals are sometimes trained with "rewards." The behavior of a hungry animal can be "rewarded" with	Food	96
2. A technical term for "reward" is reinforcement. To "reward" an organism with food is to .... it with food.	Reinforce	100
3. *Technically* speaking, a thirsty organism can be .... with water.	Reinforced	100
- - - - - - - - - - - - - -		
50. A school teacher is likely, whenever possible, to dismiss a class when her students are rowdy because she has been .... by elimination of the stimuli arising from a rowdy class.	Reinforced	92
51. The teacher who dismisses a class when it is rowdy causes the frequency of future rowdy behavior to (1) ...., since dismissal from class is probably a(n) (2) .... for rowdy children.	(1) Increase (2) Reinforcement	86
- - - - - - - - - - - - - -		
54. If an airplane spotter never sees the kind of plane he is to spot, his frequency of scanning the sky (1) .... In other words, his "looking" behavior is (2)	(1) Decreases (2) Extinguished (or: Not Reinforced)	94

withdrawal of stimulus support. This we shall call fading. This method will be illustrated with some neuroanatomy material.[1] A fully labelled cross section of the medulla oblongata is placed before the student while he works with a large set of items pertaining to the spatial arrangement of the various structures. For example, "posterior to the cuneate nuclei are the ———." The answer is: "the cuneate fasciculi."

After many such items, he begins another set and has another picture before him, but now the structures are only labelled with initials. A new set of items again asks a long series of questions pertaining to the spatial position of the various structures. For example, "between the gracile and the trigeminal nuclei are ———." The answer is the "cuneate nuclei."

After many more items, he proceeds to a new set and the next picture. This time the picture is unlabelled. Again, he goes through a series of new items, not simple repetition of the previous ones, but pertaining to the same program of the spatial location of the different structures. This set is followed by still another, but with no picture at all. He is now able to discuss the spatial position of the structures without any visual representations of the structures before him. In a sense, he has his own private map of the medulla. He may further demonstrate his newly acquired ability by accurately drawing the medulla.

The neuroanatomy example is an elaborate example of fading. Fading is also applied in a more simple form in constructing verbal programs without pictorial displays. A single item may in one sentence give a definition or a general law and a second sentence in that same item an example in which a key word is omitted. This would be followed by a new example in the next frame, but with the definition or law lacking.

This brings us to our fifth principle, control of the student's observing and echoic behavior. In the classroom the student is often treated as though he were some kind

[1] This material was prepared by D. M. Brethower in collaboration with the present author and is being used at Harvard for research purposes.

of passive receiver of information who can sop up information spoken by the teacher, written on the blackboard, or presented by films. But all of these are effective only insofar as the student has some behavior with respect to the material. He must listen carefully, or read carefully, thus engaging in usually covert echoic behavior.

Ineffectiveness of classroom techniques is often credited to "inattention" or poor "concentration." It has been shown (Reid, 1953) that if a discrimination is to be learned, adequate observing behavior must first be established. We have further found (Holland, 1958) that observing behavior, or, speaking loosely, "attention" is subject to the same forms of control as other behavior. This control of observing behavior is of prime importance. When the student becomes very "inattentive" in the classroom, the teaching material flows on; but with a machine, he moves ahead only as he finishes an item. Lapses in active participation result in nothing more than the machine sitting idle until the student continues.

There is, however, a more subtle aspect to the control of observing behavior than this obvious mechanical one. In many of the examples we have seen, success in answering the problem only depends on the student's careful observation of the material in front of him at the moment. This may be illustrated by more material from the psychology program. A graph showing stimulus generalization data is in front of the student while he works on the machine. In the program he may complete a statement like the following: "As the wave length changes in either direction from the wave length present during reinforcement, the number of responses _____." The answer is "decreases." The item serves only to control the behavior of observing the data. Of course, many more such items are used to discuss the same data.

This principle of controlled observation extends to the details of writing a single item. For example, "Two events may have a common effect. An operant reinforced with two reinforcers appropriate to different deprivations will vary with _____ deprivations." The answer is "two" or "both." Here the programmer's choice of the omission serves to insure a careful reading of the item. *Only* those parts of an item which must be read to correctly complete a blank can safely be assumed to be learned.

Our sixth principle deals with discrimination training. In learning spoken languages, for example, it is necessary to be able to identify the speech sounds. A student may listen to a pair of words on a special phonograph which repeats the passage as many times as he desires. The visual write-in machine instructs him to listen to a specific passage. For example, the student may hear two words such as: "sit, set." He listens as many times as he needs, then writes the phonetic symbols in the write-in machine and operates the machine, thereby exposing the true answer and providing immediate reinforcement for his correct discrimination.

However, little academic education is *simple* discrimination. More often, it is abstraction or concept formation. An abstraction is a response to a single isolated property of a stimulus. Such a property cannot exist alone. Redness is an abstraction. Anything that is red has other properties as well—size, shape, position in space, to name a few. There are red balls, red cars, red walls. The term "red" applies to all of them but not to green balls, blue cars, or yellow walls. To establish an abstraction (Hovland, 1953), we must provide many examples; each must have the common property, but among the various examples there must be a wide range of other properties. This is best illustrated by examples from a preverbal machine.

These examples are from a program[2] which teaches a child to respond to the abstract property of form. In each item, the upper figure is the sample and the lower three are the alternatives. While developing a program for establishing an abstraction we remember our earlier principles, and move through a gradual progression. For the first several items there is a sample and a single match, the other two being blank. The sample and its match are exactly alike at this stage.

After many such items, we would begin to have others in which the sample and its match again correspond in size, color and form, but an additional incorrect alterna-

[2] The program was prepared by B. F. Skinner.

tive has been added which differs from the sample in all these aspects. Later we move on to frames with three choices, again the sample and its match corresponding exactly. Next, the sample and the match may differ in some property such as color or size. It is essential that the program contain many items among which the sample and correct match differ in all properties except the one providing the basis for the abstraction. Otherwise the abstraction will be incomplete because the extraneous property will share some of the control over the abstract response.

As we move on with additional examples, the sample and the correct match differ both in color and in size, and the incorrect alternatives are beginning to share some of the extraneous properties with the sample. The student continues with many such problems in which the only common property between the sample and the correct match is the shape, regardless of size and color. Even now our abstraction may be incomplete. We have kept the figures in only one orientation. Therefore, we also have a series in which the samples are rotated.

A great deal of academic education consists of trying to teach abstractions. Concepts such as force, reinforcement, supply-and-demand, freedom, and many, many other possible examples are all abstractions. Furthermore, in the academic setting, the student seldom adequately forms abstractions. The trigonometry student commonly uses triangles with the right angle as one of the two lower angles. If the triangle is rotated 90°, so that the right angle is upward, the student often does not recognize it as a right triangle. Neither is an abstraction developed simply by learning a definition. The psychology student who learns the definition of reinforcement in formal terms and is acquainted with a laboratory example of food reinforcement, may not realize the horrible consequences of sending his girl friend flowers to end an argument. Thus, in the psychology program, to develop a new concept, we follow the pattern in the preverbal example. A wide range of examples are analyzed which differ in as many aspects as possible, each still having the common property which characterizes the concept.

The last principle I shall discuss is really a question of

methodology which has served so well in the laboratory. This principle is to let the student write the program. A few years ago, a cartoon was published in the *Columbia Jester*. The rat leaning on a bar is saying to the other rat: "Boy, do we have this guy conditioned. Every time I press the bar down, he drops a pellet in."

Although said in jest, it is true that the rat controls the experimenter's behavior. When interesting things are observed about the rat's behavior, the control circuits are rewired to investigate the interesting new facet of behavior. In a sense, the rat is wiring the control circuit. Similarly, the behavioral engineer who prepares good teaching machine material must be under the control of the student's responses. When the student has trouble with part of a program the programmer must correct this. The student's answers reveal ambiguities in items; they reveal gaps in the program and erroneous assumptions as to the student's background. The answer will show when the program is progressing too rapidly, when additional prompts are necessary, or when the programmer should try new techniques. When unexpected errors are made, they indicate deficiencies *not* in the student but in the program.

The most extensive experience with this principle of modifying the program to fit the student has been at Harvard (Holland, 1959) with the psychology program. In 1958, we had a program consisting of forty-eight disks or lessons of twenty-nine frames each. After using the program and making a detailed, item-by-item analysis of the students' answers we diagnosed the particular deficiencies in the program and revised it accordingly. The program was also extended to cover a larger amount of subject matter and, in 1959, it consisted of sixty disks. You have already seen a few items from the course. After using the revised material in 1959, we evaluated the extent of its improvement. Table 2 shows the percentage of errors on the first twenty disks for each of the two years.

The revision eliminated about half the errors. The last column of the table gives percentage of improper self-scoring by the students. Revision also cut these scoring errors approximately in half. Furthermore, the revision

TABLE 2

*A comparison of the student's errors in
using the revised (1959) and unrevised
(1958) program in psychology.*

	Per cent Errors	Per cent Items Improperly Scored by Students
1958	20.1	3.6
1959	11.0	1.4

decreased the time required to complete the material. Although the second year's material had more disks— sixty as opposed to forty-eight—it actually required the average student about one hour less to complete the work than it had required for the shorter first version. Frequency distributions on the median times in minutes for completion of the various disks are shown in Fig. 1.

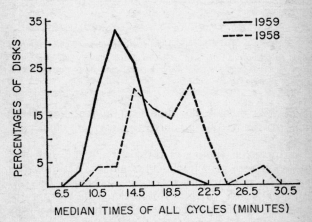

Fig. 1. *Here are the frequency distributions for the median times to complete disks or "lessons" for the revised and unrevised psychology program. Raw frequencies were converted to percentages to equate the area under the curves.*

These are the times required for the median student to move through each set of material answering every item once and to repeat the items answered incorrectly. Notice the considerable time required for many disks in the first year's material. Primarily this was because students repeated the larger number of items missed in the first cycle.

But the improved material provided faster performance, even when the delay due to repetition of incorrectly answered items is not considered. The frequency distributions for the first cycle only are provided in Fig. 2.

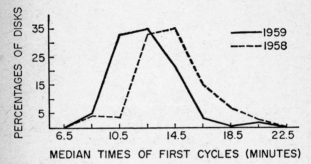

Fig. 2. Here are the frequency distributions for the median times to complete only the first cycles for the revised and unrevised psychology program. Raw frequencies were converted to percentages to equate area under the curves.

These data exclude the time used in repeating items. Here too the revision produced slightly more rapid progress.

Such careful tailoring of material to fit the student is impossible with most teaching techniques. With teaching machines, as in no other teaching technique, the programmer is able to revise his material in view of the students' particular difficulties. The student can write the program; he cannot write the textbook.

We have seen that the principles evolved from the laboratory study of behavior have provided the possibility for the behavioral engineering of teaching. This new technology is thoroughly grounded in some of the better established facts of behavioral control. The future of education is bright if persons who prepare teaching machine programs appreciate this, and appropriately educate themselves in a special, but truly *not* esoteric, discipline.

But it is vital that we continue to apply these techniques in preparing programs. The ill-advised efforts of some of our friends, who automatize their courses without adopting the new technology, have an extremely good chance of burying the whole movement in an avalanche of teaching-machine tapes.

REFERENCES

Azrin, N. H., Some effects of two intermittent schedules of immediate and non-immediate punishment, *J. Psychol.*, 1956, **42**, 3-21.

Diederich, P. B., Self-correcting homework in English. *Proceedings of the 1959 Invitational Conference on Testing Problems.* Princeton: ETS, 1960.

Hively, W., Exploratory investigation of a teaching machine for visual discrimination. In: Lumsdaine A. A. and Glaser, Robert. *Teaching Machines and Programmed Learning.* Washington, D.C.: National Education Association, 1960.

Holland, J. G., Human vigilance, *Science*, 1958, **128**, 61-67.

———, Teaching psychology by a teaching-machine program. Paper presented at the 1959 meeting of the American Psychological Association.

Holland, J. G., and Skinner, B. F., A self-tutoring introduction to a science of behavior. Unpublished manuscript; copies available.

Homme, L. E., and Glaser, R., Relationship between the programmed textbook and teaching machines. Paper presented at the Conference on Automatic Teaching of Verbal and Symbolic Skills, 1958.

Hovland, C. I., A "communication analysis" of concept learning, *Psychol. Rev.*, 1952, **59**, 461-472.

———, A set of flower designs for experiments in concept formation, *Amer. J. Psychol.*, 1953, **66**, 140-142.

Keller, F. S., and Schoenfeld, W. N. *Principles of Psychology.* New York: Appleton, 1950.

Perin, C. T., The effect of delayed reinforcement upon the differentiation of bar responses in white rats, *J. Exptl. Psychol.*, 1943, **32**, 95-109.

Pressey, S. L., Simple apparatus which gives tests and scores and teaches, *School and Society*, 1926, **23**, 373-376.

Reid, L. S., The development of noncontinuity behavior through continuity learning, *J. Exptl. Psychol.*, 1953, **46**, 107-112.

SKINNER, B. F., The science of learning and the art of teaching, *Harvard Ed. Rev.*, 1954, **29**, 86-97.

————. *Verbal Behavior.* New York: Appleton, 1957.

————, Teaching machines, *Science*, 1958, **128**, 969-977.

WYCKOFF, L. B., The role of observing responses in discrimination learning, *Psychol. Rev.*, 1952, **59**, 431-442.

4

Skinner's Theory of Teaching Machines*

DAVID ZEAMAN

University of Connecticut

One of the differences between the natural and the social sciences is that in the natural sciences, each succeeding generation stands on the shoulders of those that have gone before, while in the social sciences, each generation steps in the faces of its predecessors.

Whether psychology is a natural science or an unnatural one may be a question, but given a practical psychological problem of training devices to solve, there is no question at all that we have a choice of two strategies here, the shoulder or the face.

If it is the shoulder, where should the constructor and the programmer of human training devices look in the scientific literature of psychology for experimental data relevant to his task?

Any answer to this question implies a theory of training devices. It is in this loose but yet important sense that the word theory is here used.

Skinner has a theory, if I read him rightly, and it says the appropriate reference class of experiments, the appropriate experimental paradigm, for construction and

---

* This article originally appeared in Eugene Galanter (Ed.), *Automatic Teaching: The State of the Art.* New York: John Wiley & Sons, Inc., 1959, Chapter 14. It is used here with the permission of the author and the publisher.

programming teaching machines is that of free operant conditioning. Others, in particular those using the memory drum, are held to be inappropriate.

Skinner's resolution of the shoulder-face question is, happily, the shoulder, but the shoulders are too ivy-league-ish—too narrow.

It is the counter-thesis of this talk, that existing teaching machines (and those likely soon to be built) represent complex admixtures of at least three basic experimental paradigms, free operant, controlled operant, and classical conditioning, and that of these, the free operant may be the least pertinent. Furthermore, of all the commonly used apparatuses for experimental study of learning that one which most closely resembles one of Skinner's teaching machines (the Write-in Model) is the memory drum.

Since there is something less than universal agreement on classification of learning paradigms, let me ask for a temporary convention in the use of the words "controlled operant, free operant, and classical conditioning."

All three refer to experimental arrangements of observable variables that a machine can handle. The common elements of all three include two stimulus events S_1 and S_2, occurring in that order, and at least two responses arbitrarily designated as correct and incorrect.

By "controlled operant" or "discrete trial operant" is meant those experiments incorporating the following acquisition features: (keeping the Graham-Gagne Runway experiments in mind will help you here).

The acquisition trial begins with the presentation of a stimulus situation S_1 which lasts until the subject makes a correct response—R. One and *only* one correct response R occurs per trial because the correct response terminates S_1. It also brings S_2, which in this case is a reinforcing stimulus. S_2 does *not* elicit R. The timing arrangements are partially subject controlled, partially experimenter. The time interval between S_1 and S_2 is subject controlled since S_2 is contingent upon R, but the intertrial interval, that is the $S_2 - S_1$ interval is usually under the experimenter's control.

Acquisition is measured by S-R latency or the conditional probability of R given S_1.

Illustrative apparatuses for controlled operant conditioning include the runway, Miller-Mowrer Shuttle Box, Retractible Bar Skinner Box, the Single-door Lashley Jumping Stand, and also if correction technique is used, the Simple T-Maze, Discrimination Boxes and the Two-door Jumping Stand.

In the free operant or ordinary Skinner box situation, similar features are present with some exceptions. The initial stimulus situation S_1 is of prolonged duration, allowing many correct responses to occur, each one reinforced during continuous acquisition by the contingent reinforcing stimulus S_2. This of course permits a rate measure to be taken.

Both the free and controlled operant paradigms, then, display an SRS sequence, with the second S contingent upon R. The big difference lies in the number of correct responses allowed per trial, only one in the controlled operant (since the correct response eliminated S_1 as well as bringing S_2), but *many* correct responses in the free operant.

What about timing differences? Is one self-paced and the other not? If one accepts Estes' analysis of the free operant, the animal turns S_1 on and off by himself, even though the experimenter leaves it on. Each reinforcing stimulus S_2 turns over the S_1 and the subject gets a fresh look at S_1. In this analysis, the free operant is self-paced, in the sense that the subject controls the intertrial interval, the time between S_2 and S_1.

This is to be contrasted with the controlled operant in which the subject waits for the experimenter to turn on S_1. It is not completely self-paced.

It is important to note here that if you accept this analysis and regard the free operant as self-paced, it is only so when the S_1's remain the same.

If the experimenter has a number of different S_1's to be connected to a number of different correct responses, free operant techniques can be used, but then it is no longer completely self-paced. The experimenter changes the problem. The inter-problem interval is not subject controlled, and it is this interval that we are usually interested in with teaching machines.

Now finally to the classical conditioning paradigm.

The previous two paradigms were SRS sequences with a contingency. This one is an SSR sequence with no contingency. To fulfill the paradigm, the first stimulus S_1 must *not* elicit R as strongly as you would wish, whereas the second stimulus S_2 *must* elicit R, the correct response.

This is a highly operational, non-theoretical specification of the classical conditioning paradigm. It is not asserted that S_2 be an innate elicitor of R, nor even a strong stimulus. Whether such a paradigm always provides the necessary or sufficient conditions for learning is an empirical question not easily resolved, given the existing literature. It is, however, a paradigm that can be used in construction of training devices, and it looks operationally at least to be different from free and controlled operant conditioning, in not having a contingent S_2 and in requiring S_2 to elicit the correct response.

In the matter of timing, classical conditioning resembles the controlled operant in that the experimenter controls the inter-trial interval (the S_2, S_1 gap) but classical conditioning differs from both free and controlled operants in also giving control over the $S_1 - S_2$ interval to the experimenter.

With these three paradigms specified in this way, let us take a look at three pieces of apparatus, a memory drum set up for paired associates, Skinner's Write-in Model teaching machine and Skinner's Arithmetic machine.

First the paired associates experiment. On the first trial around, there is ordinarily no anticipation. The subject sees the S_1 syllable and reads the correct associate. This fits the classical conditioning paradigm. It is an SSR sequence, no contingency, and all stimulus intervals under control of the experimenter.

On the second and subsequent trials, the possibility of operant conditioning enters. If the subject correctly anticipates the associate, he is reinforced by the match of his anticipated answer and the forced answer. Since this matching or knowledge of correct results, is contingent upon a correct anticipation, elements of a controlled operant are present.

If the subject gives the wrong response, the contingent reinforcement is not present, and the trial resembles an extinction trial of a controlled operant. The trial ends, of course, with a classical conditioning feature, a forcing of the correct response, elicited by the appearance of the associate.

If no overt response is given at all, the trial becomes a simple classical conditioning trial again.

Thus there are three kinds of trials possible with a paired associates machine, a simple classical trial, a controlled operant acquisition trial with a terminal classical feature, or a controlled operant extinction trial with a terminal classical feature. The timing of these trials is almost exclusively that of a classical conditioning, however both the $S_1 - S_2$ interval *and* the $S_2 - S_1$ interval are experimenter controlled. To my knowledge there are no animal experiments with trials at all like these, although I believe they might be arranged.

Consider now Skinner's Write-in Model learning machine. It presents a written question or an incompleted sentence or paragraph in an aperture, and then waits for the subject to write in his answer or completion. Following this the subject operates the machine to present the correct written answer to be compared with his own. The next problem appears when the subject indicates to the machine that he is ready.

We analyze the machine in the terms used before. As with the memory drum there are three kinds of trials, depending upon whether the subject makes no response, makes the correct response, or makes an incorrect response.

If no response is made, the trial looks like a classical conditioning paradigm or SSR. The question stimulus S_1 is presented. Then the answer stimulus follows, and elicits the answer response. No contingency, just a forced response like classical conditioning.

If the correct response is made, an instrumental or operant feature emerges. The correct answer given in anticipation of S_2 is reinforced by a matching of the correct results. This reinforcement is of course contingent, and makes the trial resemble the free *or* controlled operant. But since there is only one correct response made, this aspect of the trial looks most like the controlled operant.

If an *incorrect* response is made, the contingent matching reinforcement is absent and we have elements of a controlled operant extinction trial. The trial is terminated however with the forced response characteristic of the classical procedure.

The high similarity of these three kinds of trials with those of the paired associates memory drum experiment is obvious. Yet there is some difference. A difference in timing. With the usual paired associates procedure, all stimulus intervals are *experimenter* controlled. With the Write-in Model, in contrast, the $S_1 - S_2$ interval is *subject* controlled (that is, the subject can give himself as much time as he wants before presenting S_2) and the interproblem interval is also subject controlled. It is indeed a self-paced device.

The subject's control of the timing of the S_2 stimulus is by no means new: it is a property of free and controlled operant procedures in general, but the subject's control of the interproblem interval is relatively novel. It is *not* found in either the usual controlled operant experiment, or in the usual free operant, nor of course, in classical conditioning. Some recent experiments on the role of observing responses in animal discrimination have incorporated an analogous type of paradigm. Wyckoff had pigeons turning on their own discriminative stimuli by stepping on a treadle. His work should be relevant to this machine. And other work may be relevant too.

Since there have been so many memory drum experiments done, and since it is no engineering trick at all to convert the usual memory drum to an entirely self-paced apparatus, like Skinner's Write-in Model, I would be surprised if a literature survey failed to turn up any self-paced paired associates data. Of course when a subject riffles through a deck of flash cards at his own time, the paradigm for this primitive machine is the same as that of Skinner's Write-in Model.

The last device to be inspected is a modification of one of Skinner's devices which we have also constructed and called the "Arithmachine." It presents visual material and allows the subject to make any of a large number of numerical responses, one of which is correct. The response is the movement of sliders and the turning of a crank. If the sliders have been positioned correctly, each slider position representing a number, the turning of the crank will bring reinforcement and the next problem.

The analysis. This machine operation looks much more like the controlled operant procedure than does the Write-in Model. The S_1 or question is presented, a response is waited for, and a contingency set up. If the response is correct, the subject is rewarded by the complete turning of the crank and whatever other reinforcing signals the experimenter wants. There are no forced responses of a classical nature at the end of the trial. The correct response not only brings reinforcement, it eliminates S_1, the question stimulus, thus allowing only one correct response per trial, the hallmark of the controlled operant.

Timing is not completely self-paced. The $S_1 - S_2$ interval is subject controlled, but the interproblem interval is not. The problems come in massed sequence. As soon as the subject finds out that he has been right on the last problem, the new one stares up at him.

Strength of acquisition is inferred with this apparatus from latency or probability of response, as it is for the other machines mentioned. Free rate of operant response, in the presence of a prolonged S_1 is not taken here, nor is it a measure taken for any teaching machine that I know of.

This machine, in summary, embodies all of the elements of the controlled operant, and the literature on this kind of experiment may therefore be relevant.

In final summary, the original question is re-asked, where should the constructor and programmer of human training devices look in the scientific literature of psychology for experimental data relevant to his task. Any answer to this question implies a theory of training devices. If Skinner's theory says that the literature on free operant is most relevant, this paper proposes the counter theory that the literature of controlled operant and classical conditioning is also relevant but more so.

If Skinner's theory says that memory drum experiments provide an inappropriate model for construction of training devices, this paper proposes the counter theory that no other experimental device or procedure more closely resembles Skinner's Write-in Machine than a common memory drum paradigm.

Old Ebbinghaus's shoulders may not be ivy-league, but we ought to stand on them anyway.

PARADIGMS

A) *Controlled Operant*

       Trial 1   Trial 2

S_1 R S_2 S_1 R S_2

  Subject   Experimenter

  Controlled   Controlled

B) *Free Operant*

               Trial 1   Trial 2

   S_1 R S_2 R S_2 R S_2 S_1 R S_2 R S_2 R S_2

   Subject   Experimenter

  Controlled   Controlled

C) *Classical Conditioning*

       Trial 1   Trial 2

S_1 S_2 R S_1 S_2 R

 Experimenter   Experimenter

  Controlled   Controlled

5

A Review of the Literature on Certain Aspects of Automated Instruction*

W. J. CARR

Temple University

The primary purpose of this paper is to review the fast-growing literature on the design and utility of automatic teaching devices. A secondary purpose of the paper is to suggest a number of hypotheses, the testing of which might further our understanding of the variables which influence the effectiveness of automated instruction in the classroom.

The plan of the present paper is as follows: First, there will be an attempt to provide a conceptual framework in which to place a discussion of automatic teaching devices. Second, a review will be made of the rather extensive literature on automated instruction. In this section, the writer will be concerned with two types of studies,

* A report submitted (January 1959) to Dr. J. Charles Jones, Director, Susquehanna Valley Program, Bucknell University. Support for this work was received from a grant from the Fund for the Advancement of Education to Bucknell University. The report is used here with the permission of the author. Similar versions of this paper have appeared in Lumsdaine, A. A., and Glaser, Robert (Ed.), *Teaching Machines and Programmed Learning*, Washington, D.C.: National Education Association, 1960, and WADC Technical Report 59-503, Air Research and Development Command (August 1959).

(a) simple evaluation studies, in which the researcher compared the effectiveness of a given teaching device with the "standard" form of instruction and (b) parametric studies, in which the researcher investigated one or more variables of which the effectiveness of the teaching device might be a function. Finally, there will be an attempt to summarize some of the current thinking as to how research in this area might best proceed and to suggest some specific hypotheses.

SOME PRINCIPLES OF LEARNING

For almost one hundred years, psychologists have expended a considerable portion of their research effort toward an understanding of the learning process, chiefly by studying the variables which influence the rate of learning and forgetting. Out of this effort has come a number of reliable principles of learning which can be utilized to design an efficient learning situation.

Gagne (1958) has reviewed the literature on learning, on a very broad scale. His paper encompasses almost all of the known variables which influence learning and retention. Moreover, Gagne has discussed at some length the importance of using adequate measures of learning, which necessarily includes the problem of transfer from the classroom to real life.

Skinner (1954) and Gilbert (1958) have summarized those principles of learning which have led a number of workers to consider seriously the development of automatic teaching devices for use in the classroom. A rephrasing of these principles, couched in non-technical terms, might take the following form. Accompanying each principle is a brief statement showing how that principle is sometimes violated in the typical classroom.

1. *Learning takes place most rapidly if the student is actively engaged with the subject matter.* At the outset of training, some time might profitably be spent in watching or listening to someone else perform the acts to be learned, but the student will become proficient only if he practices the acts himself. This principle applies to verbal skills as well as to non-verbal ones. Unfor-

tunately, in most classrooms the learning of most subject matter is thought of as being a spectator, rather than a participator sport.

2. *Learning is most effective if the student develops the skills and knowledge in a form which will readily generalize to the "real life" situation for which they are intended.* Usually, this means that the student must learn to construct correct answers to questions, rather than merely be able to recognize them. Thus, the responses which the student makes in the learning situation should be of the former rather than of the latter type. All too frequently, in the classroom of today, recognition is used as a criterion of learning.

3. *Learning takes place most rapidly if* immediate *"knowledge of results"* [1] *is given for each response.* If the response is correct, the student should be so informed, just as soon as the response is completed. If the response is incorrect, he should know this, also. Even a slight delay drastically retards learning. Presently, our students must frequently endure long delays before they receive feedback of this sort.

4. *Learning takes place most rapidly if the subject matter is organized in a hierarchic form.* Lessons should begin with very simple problems, for which the student already has the necessary skills and knowledge. Gradually, the difficulty level may be raised until the desired level of proficiency is obtained. Care must be exercised so that at each point the student is given new information to be used to solve the next problem. Ideally, the subject matter should be presented in steps so small that the success of the student on the next problem is practically guaranteed. Unfortunately, both textbooks and classroom techniques frequently ignore this principle.

5. *Receiving frequent "knowledge of results" keeps students working at the assigned task.* The hurdles which the student must surmount should be kept immediately

---

[1] The sophisticated reader will recognize that mere "knowledge of results" does not guarantee rapid learning. Strictly speaking, learning takes place only if the "knowledge of results" also constitutes reinforcement. A reinforcement is a stimulus which increases the probability of the stimulus-response connection which it follows.

before him and by making successes frequent, the student will develop a high level of aspiration. In the typical classroom, the student is studying to prepare himself for a far-off quiz or test. The result is that the teacher must spend a considerable portion of her time devising some artificial motivators, to keep the students working.

6. *Since learning takes place in individuals, the learning situation should be designed so that each student may proceed at his own pace.* For various reasons, some students learn faster than others and therefore, it is difficult to have them learn in groups.[2] This principle does not necessarily dictate that students must work alone. It merely emphasizes the belief that if students are to learn in groups, the learning situation should be designed so that the fast learners are not impeded by the slow ones and the slow learners are not confused by too stiff a pace.

The list of principles given above is neither new nor exhaustive. Good teachers have known of theses principles for a long time and have endeavored to utilize them as best they can, within the limitations of the present-day classroom situation.

But it must be recognized that the limitations imposed on the teacher by the present-day classroom situation are extremely severe. Many educators and psychologists have been impressed with the folly of trying to teach thirty or more children, simultaneously. Consider, for example, the teaching of the multiplication tables. While one student recites, the teacher is able to reinforce each of his responses. But the other children are merely listening and probably little learning occurs. Further, if the teacher uses the weekly quiz as a learning device, learning suffers from the long delay between the responses and the knowledge of results. Finally, if the class is working on the "five" tables, some bright students might more profitably be working on the "sevens" while some of the slower ones should still be working on the "threes." True, making the class more homogeneous with respect to mathematical ability might help, but this poses special administrative problems.

[2] The writer recognizes that the development of some skills requires the presence of a group. In this discussion we have reference to those skills and knowledge which do not.

The teacher's inability to work efficiently with more than a very few studetns at a time has caused a number of psychologists to follow the lead of Sidney L. Pressey and B. F. Skinner in recommending a thorough investigation of teaching by means of automatic teaching devices. Presumably, each student would have the daily use of a machine for a period of time. Theoretically, at least, the machine could be designed so that its operation would be congruent with all of the principles of efficient learning which have been here reviewed.

Skinner (1958) has discussed some of the social and economic ramifications of his proposal to make wide use of automatic teaching devices in our educational system. Space will not be devoted to this topic in the present paper, except to point out that few if any workers in this field intend to build devices designed to replace the teacher in the classroom. At the very best, the devices can only hope to supplement the efforts of the teacher, by relieving her of the task at which she is probably least capable—delivering "knowledge of results" rapidly to her students for each response directed toward the subject matter. If effective, the use of such devices would free the teacher for tasks which she can perform well and for which no machine can replace her.

A REVIEW OF LITERATURE

Porter (1958a) has recently published an excellent review of a portion of the extensive literature dealing with the many devices which have been suggested as being useful adjuncts to the teaching process. Further, he has developed a system of classification of these devices which promises to be quite useful. He has distinguished among three classes of devices:

Stimulus Devices: Stimulus devices are those which present some information to the learner, by way of one or more sense modalities. Frequently, they show how or under what conditions something is to be done. Examples of this class of device are: models, projecting devices, phonographs, braille, and the like. It should be pointed out that while these devices do present subject matter to the learner, they do not necessarily require any action on his part and thus learning is not assured. For this reason, Porter suggests that they be thought of as teaching aids, rather than teaching devices.

Response Devices: Response devices are those which provide the learner with an opportunity to practice some activity. These devices are usually used to collect or manipulate data. Examples of this class of device are typewriters and desk calculators (as data manipulators) and the Classroom Communicator or the GSR recorder (as data collectors). Thus, a response device permits the learner to practice some activity, but it does not necessarily provide him with subject matter on which to practice. For this reason, Porter suggests that response devices also be thought of as teaching aids, rather than as teaching devices.

Stimulus-Response Devices: Stimulus-Response devices are those which both present information to the learner and also require some appropriate action on his part. Further, such devices usually respond differentially, depending upon the behavior of the learner. Examples of the stimulus-response class of device are the Pressey multiple-choice apparatus, Skinner's devices and the classical memory drum. It should be noted that the stimulus-response device more nearly simulates the role of the teacher by both presenting information to the learner and requiring some appropriate action on his part. Porter feels that these might properly be called teaching devices, since no human teacher is required to mediate relations between the machine and the learner, except to service or maintain the machine.

Further, Porter distinguished among three types of stimulus-response devices. First, there is the *simulator,* which duplicates the essential characteristics of some complex task and which requires appropriate action from time to time on the part of the learner. Ordinarily, this type of device does not provide immediate feedback. The electronic flight simulator is a good illustration of this type of device.

The second type of stimulus-response device distinguished by Porter is the *immediate reinforcer,* which not only presents the learner with a problem situation but also provides him with immediate "knowledge of results" concerning his answers. It should also be noted that this type of device is learner-paced, in that the machine's reaction is contingent upon the learner's behavior. Pressey's multiple-choice device and Skinner's teaching machine are examples of the immediate reinforcer.

The third type of stimulus-response device is what Porter called the *pacer*. A pacer is a device which presents stimulus materials for a given interval of time and then provides the appropriate response, whether or not the learner has attempted to answer. The memory drum, so frequently used in psychological research on learning phenomena, illustrates this type of device.

Of the three types of stimulus-response devices distinguished above, the one which seems to offer the most promise for use in the class is the immediate reinforcer. Simulators ordinarily do not provide immediate feedback and the operation of the pacer is independent of the behavior of the learner. Thus, these latter types of devices seem to violate one or more of the principles of learning referred to earlier. Hereafter, in the present paper, consideration will be given only to those stimulus-response devices which are of the immediate reinforcer type.

A word of caution might be added with respect to Porter's classification of learning machines. It is quite possible that a slight modification of a stimulus-device or a response-device might enable it to qualify as a stimulus-response device. Also, it is possible for both simulators and pacers to be reclassified as immediate reinforcers, if appropriate changes are introduced. Porter has classified particular devices in accordance with the design of the machine offered by its designer.

SOME HISTORY OF AUTOMATED INSTRUCTION

Perhaps the first attempt to develop an automatic teaching device was made in 1918 by English (1942). This worker constructed and tested a device by which soldiers rapidly learned to squeeze rather than jerk a rifle trigger. Knowledge of results was delivered to the soldier via a manometer attached to the trigger. However, it should be pointed out that the subject matter in this case was quite simple, consisting of a single habit.

Sidney Pressey (1950) is often credited with being the first to give serious thought to the widespread use of teaching devices in the classroom. Although, at the outset, Pressey was primarily interested in automatic testing devices, he soon discovered that students could learn by taking tests via his machines. Pressey and his students have published a good number of papers in which various designs of machine have been described and evaluated.

Basically, the type of device developed by Pressey follows the format of the multiple-choice question. The student is presented with a question and four options, only one of which is correct. He chooses an option and the device provides some immediate feedback. If the student has chosen the correct answer, the machine presents the next question. If an incorrect option is chosen, the student must continue responding until he selects the correct option.

Three different recording devices were described by Pressey and his students. They developed a punch-board device, a system using chemically treated paper, and an electrical system. See Pressey (1950) for a more complete description of each.

The type of device developed by Pressey suffers from at least two defects which seem quite important. First, the student must merely recognize the correct answer among a number of options. In many cases this format is quite unlike the real life situation for which the skills are being developed and the problem of transfer arises.[3] Second, the materials which Pressey presented were not arranged in any hierarchic fashion. The lack of carefully prepared sequence of information does violence to one of the principles of learning described earlier in this paper.

Recently, Skinner (1958b) developed a different type of teaching device which circumvents the limitations of the Pressey machines. Using the devices developed by Skinner, the learner must construct, rather than merely recognize correct answers to questions. Further, Skinner and his colleagues spent a considerable portion of their

---

[3] Kendler (1958) has discussed some of the special problems of transfer connected with teaching devices.

research time, in attempting to construct programs of subject matter, beginning with simple problems and gradually increasing complexity only as the learner demonstrates that he is ready for it. For a good illustration of what is meant by a program, see Skinner (1958a, pp. 3-7).

One of Skinner's machines is used to teach arithmetic. The learner constructs his answer by operating sliders, each of which represents a digit. In this way, the learner can construct answers up to four digits in length. For materials other than arithmetic, the learner writes out his answer. Then he may compare his answer with the correct one, merely by operating a lever. The reader can easily see that such a procedure introduces a source of error, since the learner decides whether or not his answer is correct. In some models, the machine provides for recycling of those questions which the learner had wrong on previous trials.

PARAMETERS INFLUENCING THE EFFECTIVENESS OF AUTOMATED INSTRUCTION

A good deal of the research on automated instruction has taken the form of evaluation studies, in which teaching by machine has been compared with teaching by the "usual" method. The present writer shares with Gilbert (1958, p. 29) the belief that while a certain amount of evaluation research is necessary in order to justify a continued interest in the basic concept of automated instruction, the major portion of the research effort should be devoted to an experimental analysis of the parameters which influence the effectiveness of automated instruction. This latter type of study will be discussed first.

A distinction may be drawn among three classes of variables of which the effectiveness of automated instruction might be a function. They are: characteristics of the device, of the program, and of the learner. Each of these classes of variables will be discussed in some detail and an effort will be made to summarize the pertinent research findings.

Characteristics of the Device: The reader will recall that, earlier in this paper, a teaching device was defined as a machine by which stimulus materials are presented to a learner and which requires some response on his part in order for the device to operate. Further, the type of teaching device with which this paper is primarily concerned is one which provides immediate feedback to the learner. This type of analysis permits one to discuss the characteristics of the device within the framework of a three-fold analysis:

1. *Display or input characteristics:* So many specific devices have been used by workers as means of presenting the stimulus materials that a complete classification of them is almost impossible. Suffice it to say that most workers have made use of mechanical, electrical, or optical components to present information to the learner. Two exceptions may be noted. Crowder (1958b) and Homme & Glaser (1958) have successfully presented stimulus materials in the form of a modified textbook. And Rath & Anderson (1958) have used the IBM "650" print-out.

To the writer's knowledge, no experiment has been performed which compares the efficiency of different methods of presenting stimulus materials.

2. *Response or output characteristics:* Two basically different modes of responding have been employed. Pressey, and his colleagues, and some researchers in military establishments have made heavy use of the multiple-choice or recognition mode, while Skinner and others have used the "free operant" or construction mode of responding. No study was found which permits the comparison of these two basic modes of operation.

However, Irion & Briggs (1957) have experimentally compared several variations of the multiple-choice mode of operation. The four modes compared were (a) *quiz mode:* in which the S chooses one of the responses by pressing a switch and the machine immediately indicates which of the responses was correct, (b) *modified-quiz mode:* which is identical to (a) except that a buzzer indicates that an incorrect answer was made, (c) *practice mode:* in which the S must press switches until the correct response is made, and (d) *single-try mode:* in which the

S may respond only once and then the next stimulus item is presented.

Each of the four modes of operation was employed by different groups of subjects as they learned three types of tasks: serial learning, paired-associate learning, and problem solving. The dependent variables were the number of trials required to learn the tasks to a given criterion and a measure of retention, taken two weeks after learning.

In general, the relative efficiency of the four modes of operation was in the order: quiz-mode, modified-quiz mode, practice mode, and single-try mode. The amount of difference in efficiency was a function of the type of learning task. Later, Irion & Briggs used different modes of operation within a learning situation and found no differences in amount of time to criterion.

3. *Reinforcement characteristics:* Little attention has been given to the problem of the optimal type and schedule of reinforcement to use as the means of maintaining the maximal rate of performance. Most workers report that sheer "knowledge of results" suffices to keep the learner working. Skinner (1958) reports that students work harder and longer when using the machine than they do when they merely read the textbook. The implication is that "knowledge of results" is an effective reinforcer, but it seems clear that various methods of providing feedback might very well influence the learner's performance rate. For a more complete discussion of this subject, see Porter (1957, pp. 134-136).

Characteristics of the Program: Programming refers to the arrangement of the stimulus materials in the order of presentation which will maximize the rate of acquisition of the habits to be learned. Presumably, proper programming permits the gradual shaping of the learner's responses from low to high levels of approximation of the desired responses.

It should be noted that Pressey and his group gave little attention to the problem of programming, perhaps because they were primarily interested in developing testing devices and only secondarily interested in developing teaching devices. Further, it is likely that some types of subject matter require little in the way of programming at all (e.g. trouble shooting and the identification of objects such as enemy aircraft).

But for certain kinds of complex tasks, it is likely that efficient learning can take place only if the materials are carefully programmed into a hierarchy, extending from very simple to complex habits. See Gilbert (1958) for a more complete discussion of this point.

Several problems associated with programming immediately present themselves.

1. *Extrinsic Versus Intrinsic Programming:* Of those workers interested in teaching devices, Skinner was the first to give serious attention to the matter of programming. For a given subject matter, he attempted to construct a single program, through which all learners would proceed. This type might be thought of as a straight-line program. Later, Crowder (1958a, 1958b) described another type of programming which tailors the program to the individual learner, depending upon his strengths and weaknesses (as reflected by his previous errors). Crowder's might be thought of as a branching program. The branches would permit the learner to retrace his steps back through that portion of the program which his errors indicate that he did not adequately learn. Crowder referred to his type of program as *intrinsic* and he reserved the term *extrinsic* program for the type described by Skinner.

For obvious reasons, the intrinsic program would place a special burden on both the author of the program and on the teaching device used. However, the use of an intrinsic program might very well result in a more efficient learning situation. Unfortunately, no experiment has yet been done which compares the two methods of programming directly.

2. *Size of Step:* Skinner (1958) and others feel that the most effective program is one which raises the level of the learner's proficiency by such small steps that the probability of the learner being wrong is so low as to be negligible. In fact, Skinner uses the percentage correct as a measure of the optimum size of step.

On the other hand, some have argued that the optimal size of step is the one which results in the most rapid learning to a given criterion and that this optimum can only be determined experimentally. Homme & Glaser (1958) investigated the effect of size of step upon frequency of errors and upon immediate and delayed retention. Using a single program on elementary number theory, they varied the number of steps over four values: 30, 40, 51, and 67. Presumably, the greater the number of steps, the smaller the mean size of step. Independent groups of five Ss each were used. The results showed that the smaller the step, the fewer the errors and the greater the retention. However, it is conceivable that increasing the number (and therefore decreasing the size) of steps beyond 67 might have resulted in no further change in dependent variable performance. Further, the relationship between measures of learning and size of step might interact with characteristics of the program employed. Clearly, further research is necessary before this important question can be answered unequivocally, but a start has been made.

3. *Rules or Principles of Programming:* Skinner (1958), Beck (1958), and Gilbert (1958) have described a number of rules or principles of programming. Although these rules or principles seem eminently logical, they appear to lack empirical support. Thus, they might better be thought of as hypotheses to be tested. Space does not permit a detailed discussion of these rules and the interested reader is referred to the appropriate references.

Characteristics of the Learner: A third major variable of which the effectiveness of automated instruction might be a function has to do with some characteristics of the learner. For example, one might hypothesize that the use of teaching devices might wipe out differences in achievement measures associated with intelligence or aptitude test performance. The findings of a number of experiments seem to support this hypothesis.

Porter (1958) found that the correlation between IQ and achievement in spelling was lower for a group of learners who were taught by machine than for a control group who were taught in the usual fashion. Ferster & Sapon (1958) reported similar findings on the relations between aptitude and achievement in a course in German. Finally, Lumsdaine (1958) showed that the advantage of active participation in a simple learning task decreases with increases in intelligence.

The experiments just cited might lead one to believe that superior students do not learn efficiently by machine. Pressey (1950), Briggs (1947) and Jensen (1949) have all reported data which show that bright students are quite capable of benefiting from the use of teaching devices.

Another characteristic of the learner which might influence the effectiveness of automated instruction is the level of anxiety of the learner with respect to the subject matter being taught. Porter (in a personal communication) has suggested that learners who are quite anxious or who have a low level of aspiration concerning the subject matter seem to be ones who profit a great deal from machine instruction. It seems reasonable to suppose that since the machine instruction provides for many reinforcements, the learner's degree of anxiety might be reduced and his level of aspiration raised. The result should be an increase in rate of learning, but this hypothesis has yet to be tested.

THE EVALUATION OF AUTOMATED INSTRUCTION

A good number of studies have been located which can be used to compare the effectiveness of teaching by machine with teaching by the "usual" classroom techniques. A number of these studies were performed using one or another variation of Pressey's multiple-choice type of device. All studies conclude that there is something to be gained by using machine type of instruction. Usually, the advantage is expressed in terms of the superior performance of an experimental group (those using teaching devices) over a control group.

Porter (1957, pp. 137-40) has carefully reviewed most of these studies and has pointed to a number of defects. In many of the studies cited, little if any effort was made to equate the groups for initial proficiency with respect to the subject matter, for level of motivation, for the "novelty" effect, or for the amount of time spent in study. Further, although immediate reinforcer teaching devices were used in all of these studies, it cannot be said that these studies demonstrate the superiority of immediate versus delayed reinforcement since it seems clear that the control groups received *less* reinforcement as well as delayed reinforcement.

Several evaluation studies have been performed using Skinner's type of device in which the learner constructs his answer (rather than merely identifies it) and which presents the stimulus materials in a carefully arranged hierarchic sequence. Porter (1958) has shown that the use of such a device and program for the teaching of spelling in second and sixth grade students renders them superior in spelling achievement to a control group.

Homme & Glaser (1958) recently reported a study in which comparisons were made between groups who learned by using programmed textbooks and groups who used standard textbooks. Two types of subject matter were used: sections of a statistics course and a course in the fundamentals of music reading. In both cases, the experimental groups outperformed the control groups on achievement tests. No mention is made in this study of the procedures used to equate groups for initial proficiency, amount of time spent in study, and so on.

Holland (1958) and Ferster & Sapon (1958) have also reported the results of automated instruction, using college students as subjects. Holland had students learn sections of a course in psychology and Ferster & Sapon used the subject matter of a course in German. Control group data were not reported.

On the basis of this cursory review of the validity studies, one might conclude that we are still lacking in carefully executed experiments which unequivocally demonstrate the superiority of automated instruction over the "usual" classroom procedures. And too, one might say that we know even less about *why* automated instruction might prove to be superior. It is entirely possible that all of the validity studies are dealing with a "novelty" effect. However, Porter (1958) has shown in his year long study of spelling achievement that the second semester's performance of the experimental group was just as superior to the control group as was the first semester's performance. Such evidence would suggest that if there is a "novelty" effect operating in Porter's study, it is slow in disappearing. Nevertheless, it is very clear that a great deal of additional research is in order before we can be at all confident about the superiority of automated instruction over the "usual" classroom procedure.

A FEW HYPOTHESES TO TEST

The review of the literature presented in the previous section of this paper provides a number of hypotheses which seem worth testing. This discussion of hypotheses might well be organized around the three major classes of variables of which the effectiveness of automated instruction is a function.

Characteristics of the Device: The writer shares the view expressed by Gilbert (1958a) that, for the present, most of the research on automated instruction might best be spent by studying relations between characteristics of the program and rate of learning or amount of retention. However, at least three characteristics of the teaching device might profitably be examined immediately.

HYPOTHESIS 1. *The use of self-paced instructional devices yields more rapid learning and better retention than does group-paced devices and that this relationship holds for all types of learning tasks and for all types of learners.*

Lumsdaine (1958) has suggested that group-paced devices might prove to be almost as effective as those which permit the individual learner to proceed at his own pace. Although there is good rationale for the belief that in most cases the self-paced device will prove to be the more effective of the two, this is still an empirical question. Further, the advantage of the self-paced device over the group-paced type might interact with both the nature of the task to be learned and with a number of characteristics of the learner. Finally, the advantage of the self-paced device over the group-paced device might not be great enough to warrant the accompanying increase in original and maintenance costs.

HYPOTHESIS 2. *The use of reinforcers in addition to "knowledge of results" will result in a higher rate of performance on teaching devices and perhaps render "knowledge of results" (as a reinforcement) more resistant to satiation.*

As mentioned earlier in this paper, most researchers seem to believe that mere "knowledge of results" is sufficient reinforcement to keep students working. However, it is entirely possible that prolonged exposure to such reinforcement may result in an effect akin to stimulus satiation. Porter (1957) has warned of just such a "novelty" effect.

Moreover, it may well be that the use of other reinforcers in addition to "knowledge of results" might result in an increase in rate of performance. Skinner (1954, pp. 93-94) has suggested that approval from the teacher, being permitted to engage in desired activities, successful competition with other students, and even aversive stimulation might be used to augment the reinforcing properties of "knowledge of results."

HYPOTHESIS 3. *There is an indirect relationship between the amount of delay of "knowledge of results" and the rate of learning and this relationship holds for all types of subject matter and for all types of learner.*

Pressey (1950, p. 418), in particular, has argued that the superiority of teaching devices over the more standard pedagogic practices stems from the fact that the devices minimize the delay between the learner's responses and "knowledge of results." But Porter (1957, p. 138) has pointed out that in several of Pressey's validating studies, the *amount* of "knowledge of results" varied simultaneously with the delay in "knowledge of results." Thus, we are left without knowing which of the two factors is the more important. Deese (1958, p. 199) reports a study by Saltzman which shows that a delay in "knowledge of results" can seriously hamper the learning of a rote verbal task. A delay of but six seconds resulted in a 50 per cent increase in errors.

However, it may well be that certain types of subject matter and perhaps certain types of learner might be able to withstand fairly long delays without affecting learning rate appreciably. Such information would be of some help to the designers of teaching devices.

HYPOTHESIS 4. *Having students learn to compose correct answers to questions results in faster learning, better retention, and more positive transfer to "real life" situations than does having students learn to recognize correct answers from among a number of options. Further, this relationship holds for all types of learning situations and for all types of learners.*

Skinner (1954) contends that, for most learning situations, it is more desirable to render learners capable of composing correct answers to questions, rather than make them able merely to recognize them. There are good reasons for believing that Skinner is correct on this point, but once again, this is an empirical question. Further, the advantage of composition over recognition may interact with the type of task and with characteristics of the learner.

Characteristics of the Program: As mentioned earlier in this paper, the writer believes that the usefulness of teaching devices is more a function of characteristics of the program than a function of characteristics of the device, itself. For the present, many believe that program writing is an art, which is perhaps another way of saying that we know little about the characteristics of the optimal program.

However, some program characteristics have already received some study. Crowder (1958b) has distinguished between extrinsic and intrinsic program techniques. Homme & Glaser (1958) investigated the characteristic called "size of step." Further, Beck (1958) and Gilbert (1958) have both written at length on a few principles of programming. Perhaps these principles might be put into the form of hypotheses worthy of experimental test. For these reasons, the following hypotheses are suggested:

HYPOTHESIS 5. *Intrinsic programming yields more rapid learning and better retention than does extrinsic programming. Further, this relationship holds for all types of subject matter and all types of learner.*

Once again, the reader should keep in mind the fact that although intrinsic programs might prove superior to extrinsic ones, the intrinsic type places a considerable burden upon both the program writer and upon the teaching device, itself. One way of reducing the mechanical complexity of the device would be to use a programmed textbook, intrinsically organized. Crowder (1958a, 1958b) has already put this idea to use.

HYPOTHESIS 6. *The rate of learning via automated instruction is a function of the size of step employed in the program. Further, if properly measured, the optimal size of step is a constant for all types of subject matter.*

When a student is taught a given subject matter, it is assumed that he starts off at a given level of proficiency and, after training, ends at a higher level. Now, one may attempt to go from the lower to the higher level by presenting the learner with relatively few or many steps. Further, assuming that the steps are roughly equidistant, then size of step is negatively correlated with the number of steps. Thus, both number of steps and size of step might be variables of which the rate of learning is a function.

Skinner (1958, p. 5) feels that steps should be so small that errors are rarely if ever committed. In fact, some workers feel that the percentage of errors is a measure of the worth of an item. Items which result in more than a minimum number of errors are viewed with suspicion. On the other hand, some workers feel that some percentage of error might well be built into the program and presumably this would be done by increasing the size of step in order to obtain the desired percentage of error.

The question of the optimum size or number of steps in a given program is obviously an empirical one, to be answered by experiment. Homme & Glaser (1958) have shown that increasing the number of steps (and thereby decreasing their size) resulted in more efficient learning. However, it is entirely possible that Homme & Glaser did not vary the number of steps in the program in an asymptotic function or even in a decrease in learning efficiency. Clearly, this variable is worthy of careful examination.

Finally, the writer believes that subject matter currently thought of as being difficult may simply be material which is programmed [4] in very large steps. If a technique could be developed which would permit the measurement of size of step in units which provide an equal-ratio scale, then one could test the hypothesis that the optimal size of step is a constant for all types of subject matter. Unfortunately, the writer knows of no such technique.

Characteristics of the Learner: As mentioned earlier, several studies have shown that the amount of improvement shown by students is relatively uncorrelated with their intelligence and/or aptitude for the subject matter. Such data must be interpreted carefully. They do not imply that students with low intelligence or aptitude profit more from automated instruction than do "bright" students. Rather, these findings merely state that the amount of profit is independent of such factors as intelligence and aptitude.

Researchers would do well to continue to search for characteristics of the learner which are correlated with amount of improvement. For such information would probably give us hints about the optimal design of the program, the type and schedule of reinforcement, and of the teaching device, itself.

HYPOTHESIS 7. *The rate of learning via automated instruction is a function of level of anxiety and/or level of aspiration of the learner with respect to the subject matter.*

Porter[5] has noted clinically that one benefit of automated instruction seems to stem from the fact that some learners become less anxious about their performance on the subject matter after they have used a teaching device for some time. Such an observation suggests that immediate knowledge of results and perhaps a high percentage of correct responses might be more beneficial to learners who are anxious than to those who are not.

---

[4] The reader should recognize that teachers and textbooks program material, in the sense that the material is arranged in a hierarchy conducive to rapid learning.

[5] Personal communication.

NOTES ON DIFFICULTIES INHERENT IN RESEARCH
ON AUTOMATED INSTRUCTION

Porter (1957, pp. 137-38) and Gilbert (1958, pp. 29-32) have discussed some of the difficulties inherent in research on automated instruction. Both workers feel that most evaluation studies presently available simply do not meet the necessary criteria of excellence which permit us to state categorically that automated instruction results in performance superior to instruction via the "usual" techniques. Most studies simply lack sufficient experimental control. The experimental and control groups differ in so many respects that it is impossible to tell which of the differences in treatment account for the differences in performance.

The chief difficulty seems to stem from the inability to control the subjects' previous experience with, and aptitude for, the subject matter to be learned. Most studies have used regular students as subjects in classrooms at all levels of education. Further, the subject matter employed is usually standard material. Finally, many of the studies have employed such large numbers of subjects that it is practically impossible to learn much about what is taking place while an individual is learning.

The writer suggests that at least some research time might be devoted to the careful observation of small numbers of subjects while they are learning materials with which they are totally unfamiliar. The classical nonsense syllable or objects frequently used in concept formation studies recommend themselves. Zeaman (1958) recently discussed the use of the latter type of material within the context of automated instruction.

If, for one reason or another, the researcher desires to do research in a real classroom, he might give thought to the teaching of relatively discrete skills which are subject matter for only one or two years of schooling. For example, at the elementary school level one might easily program the teaching of "telling time" or the use of roman numerals. Such instruction rarely interacts with other types of subject matter. At the collegiate level, the teaching of parliamentary rules might be more easily programmed than the teaching of algebra, philosophy, and the like.

Further, ease of programming is not the only benefit which might obtain from the use of subject matter described above. Since such material is relatively discrete, the techniques used to teach it will not interact with the learning of other subject matter.

REFERENCES

BECK, J., On some methods of programming. Paper read at the Air Force Office of Scientific Research and the Univ. of Penna. Conference on the Automatic Teaching of Verbal and Symbolic Skills, Philadelphia, December, 1958.

BRIGGS, L. J., Intensive classes for superior students. *J. Educ. Psychol.*, 1947, **38**, 207-215.

CROWDER, N. A., Intrinsically programmed materials for teaching complex skills and concepts. Paper read at the Amer. Psychol. Ass., Washington, D.C., August, 1958. (a)

———, Automatic tutoring by means of intrinsic programming. Paper read at the Air Force Office of Scientific Research and the Univ. of Penna. Conference on the Automatic Teaching of Verbal and Symbolic Skills, Philadelphia, December, 1958. (b)

DEESE, J. *The Psychology of Learning.* New York: McGraw-Hill, 1958.

ENGLISH, H. B., How psychology can facilitate military training —a concrete example, *J. Appl. Psychol.*, 1942, **26**, 3-7.

FERSTER, C. B., and SAPON, S. M., An application of recent developments in psychology to the teaching of German, *Harv. Educ. Rev.*, 1958, **28**, 58-69.

GAGNE, R. M. *A review of factors in learning efficiency.* AFOSR-TN-58-294. Air Force Office of Scientific Research. Air Research and Development Command. U.S. Air Force. Washington 25, D.C., November 1958.

GILBERT, T. F., An early approximation to principles of programming continuous-discourse, self-instructional materials. A report to Bell Telephone Laboratories, Inc., Murray Hill, N.J., September 1958.

HOMME, L., and GLASER, R., Relationships between the programmed textbook and teaching machines. Paper read at the Air Force Office of Scientific Research and the Univ. of Penna. Conference on the Automatic Teaching of Verbal and Symbolic Skills, Philadelphia, December 1958.

HOLLAND, J. G., A teaching machine program in psychology and its classroom use. Paper read at the Air Force Office of Scientific Research and the Univ. of Penna. Conference on the Automatic Teaching of Verbal and Symbolic Skills, Philadelphia, December 1958.

IRION, A. L., and BRIGGS, L. J. *Learning task and mode of operation variables in the use of the subject-matter trainer.* AFPTRC-TR-57-8. Air Force Personnel & Training Research Center. Lackland Air Force Base, Texas, October 1957.

JENSEN, B. T., An independent study laboratory using a self-scoring test, *J. Educ. Research*, 1949, **43**, 134-147.

KENDLER, H., Teaching machines and psychological theory. Paper read at the Air Force Office of Scientific Research and the Univ. of Penna. Conference on the Automatic Teaching of Verbal and Symbolic Skills, Philadelphia, December 1958.

LUMSDAINE, A. A., Partial and more complete automation of teaching processes: some psychological and economic considerations. Paper read at the Air Force Office of Scientific Research and the Univ. of Penna. Conference on the Automatic Teaching of Verbal and Symbolic Skills, Philadelphia, December 1958.

PORTER, D., A critical review of a portion of the literature on teaching devices *Harv. Educ. Rev.*, 1957, **27**, 126-147.

———, Douglas Teaching Machines, *Harv. Grad. Sch. of Educ. Ass. Bull.*, 1958, Vol. **3**. No. 1. (a)

———, Some effects of year-long teaching machine instruction in an elementary school. Paper read at the Air Force Office of Scientific Research and the Univ. of Penna. Conference on the Automatic Teaching of Verbal and Symbolic Skills, Philadelphia, December 1958. (b)

PRESSEY, S. S., Development and appraisal of devices providing immediate scoring of objective tests and concomitant self-instruction, *J. Psychol.*, 1950, **29**, 417-447.

RATH, G., and ANDERSON, N. S., The IBM research center teaching machine project: (1) the teaching of binary arithmetic; and (2) the simulation of a binary arithmetic teaching machine of the IBM 650. Paper read at the Air Force Office of Scientific Research and the Univ. of Penna. Conference on the Automatic Teaching of Verbal and Symbolic Skills, Philadelphia, December 1958.

SKINNER, B. F., Science of learning and the art of teaching, *Harv. Educ. Rev.*, 1954, **24**, No. 2, 86-97.

———, Teaching machines, *Science*, 1958, **128**, 969-977. (a)

———, *The use of teaching machines in college instruction.* Final report to the Fund for the Advancement of Education, August 15, 1958. (b)

ZEAMAN, D., Skinnerian theory and teaching machines. Paper read at the Air Force Office of Scientific Research and the Univ. of Penna. Conference on the Automatic Teaching of Verbal and Symbolic Skills, Philadelphia, December 1958.

6

Teaching Machine Dichotomy: Skinner vs. Pressey*

EDWARD B. FRY

Loyola University, Los Angeles

Even though the field of teaching machines is not very old or very large, there has already developed what appears to be a relatively major dichotomy. On one hand we have the historically older faction headed by Sidney Pressey at Ohio State University, which emphasizes multiple-choice devices; and on the other, a newer faction headed by B. F. Skinner at Harvard University, which emphasizes construction of response devices. Numerous theoretical and practical considerations (amount of error permitted and methods of programming) enter into the dichotomy.

The common characteristics of teaching machines may be described simply. These are devices which tutor the student without assistance from a human instructor. They require the student's active participation. He must respond to questions which may be interspersed with graphic or verbal subject matter, or with other techniques as the Socratic method or "vanishing" (gradually removing part of a word or phrase until the student responds

* Paper presented at the annual convention of the American Psychological Association, Cincinnati, September 1959. This article originally appeared in *Psychological Reports*, 1960, **6,** 11-14, and is used here with the permission of the author and the editor.

without a cue). Two basic principles are involved: (a) *complete variability in rate*, rate being determined by the student's responses which permit individual differences, and (b) *immediate knowledge of results*, i.e., the device "rewards" the student with the answer immediately after he responds.

TYPES OF QUESTIONS AND LEARNING THEORY

The first major difference between the two schools is the type of questions preferred. Pressey prefers the multiple-choice type of question, partly because originally he envisioned his teaching machine as also an automatic testing device. He states (1926) that permitting the student to make more than one error per question (his "degree of ignorance" per question) greatly increases the spread and significance of the total score. Learning theory at that time was strongly influenced by associationism. Pressey referred to the laws of recency, frequency, and effect, but was also willing to use questions which called for "insight."

Skinner prefers that the student construct his answers rather than relying upon recognition. On his arithmetic machine (1954) the student responds by moving digit-marked sliders to indicate the correct answer. The constructed-response type of question is in line with Skinner's emphasis on the principle of operant conditioning in which characteristic learning is controlled by rewarding the student after he has made the correct response. Skinner attempts to structure the situation so that responses lead step by step toward the desired goal, thus shaping behavior through successive approximations.

AMOUNT OF ERROR DESIRABLE

Skinner would avoid the structuring of wrong answers in programming questions for his teaching machine. "Why cause any learning at all between the wrong answer and the right question?" he asks. He would be happy if every student got every question correct.

Pressey, on the other hand, is willing to allow some error. Although specific amounts of error are seldom mentioned, Pressey would say (and most psychologists would agree) that the number of right responses should greatly exceed the number of wrong.

SUPPLEMENT OR REPLACE OTHER TEACHING METHODS?

Although perhaps a debatable point, the dichotomy extends to the instructional uses planned for the two types of machines, Pressey's devices having been used more as supplemental adjuncts to courses and textbooks, and Skinner's as replacement for texts and classroom instruction. For example, Porter (1958) used a simple write-in machine to supplant spelling instruction; "No spoken instruction was given." By contrast, Pressey (1950) used multiple-choice questions with self-scoring punchboards to supplement regular instruction in educational psychology. [Incidentally, results of both studies favored the experimental groups. Neither Pressey nor Skinner would eliminate teachers, both being interested in making more efficient use of the teacher's time in class.]

IS INTELLIGENCE STRICTLY QUANTITATIVE?

To Skinner, the difference between a bright and a dull student is largely one of quantity of learning. If teaching steps are small and understandable, a poor student can learn the same thing as a bright student; he just has to work longer. And when students find concepts difficult, Skinner believes (1958), the instructor has not presented the steps in small enough or correctly ordered units. In planning curriculum, the programmer must discover and properly order the units of information, or steps.

While Pressey does not deny the truth of Skinner's quantitative concepts of intelligence and learning, his experiments are structured as though "superior" students were, indeed, different (Briggs, 1949; Jensen, 1949). Crowder (1958) actually presents more and different steps for poorer students. Pressey places no stress on the smallness of the learning steps or the ordering of presentation.

PRACTICAL APPLICATIONS

While both sides of the dichotomy envision wide use for their devices, actual hardware and experimental studies are rather scarce. Pressey showed an actual multiple-choice testing and teaching machine at the 1924 American Psychological Association meeting. And, from time to time variations have appeared, such as Peterson's chemo-card in 1931 and Angell's punchboard study (1949) in which 81 matched pairs of chemistry students used punchboards on regular quizzes. Angell and Troyer later developed a commercial punchboard which Science Research Associates published for a time. Pressey's 1950 study of over 1000 students using punchboards led to the production of the punchboard for use in the Navy (Hill, 1955).

Besnard, Briggs, and Walker (1955) developed for the Air Force several large multiple-choice devices for trouble-shooting. Electronics trouble-shooting research has produced numerous other multiple-choice devices, such as the Tab Test (Glaser, 1954), Trainer Tester, and Automat. Also, Skinner has a small battery of disc-type write-in machines which were used by Holland (1958). The Navy Special Devices Center has recently constructed a small battery of similar machines. Skinner has a slider-type of arithmetic-spelling machine produced by IBM. Also at Harvard, Porter has several of the very simple write-in machines mentioned earlier.

DICHOTOMY IN NON-MECHANICAL DEVICES

A new development is not to use machines at all, but to use books and paper devices. Although lacking some of the control of machines, these devices provide flexibility of rate, unit presentation, and immediate knowledge of results. Yet non-mechanical devices fall into the basic dichotomy discussed here. An example of a new multiple-choice paper device is Crowder's (1958) scrambled book, in which a bit of information is followed by a multiple-choice question. The student answers the question by turning to the appropriate page; the answer page tells whether the choice was correct, and why. If the

answer was wrong, further instruction is given, followed
by a new question. If correct, the next problem is presented.

Ferster and Sapon (1958) describe a cardboard device
which requires free response. A cardboard sleeve contains
a slot which exposes one line of a question on a printed
paper slip. The student writes his answer on a scrap of
paper, moves the cardboard down one line to expose the
answer, scores himself, and proceeds to the next question.
Another device is that developed by Homme, Glaser, and
Evans (1958), a "programmed textbook" to which the
student makes numerous subjective responses. He is given
the answer on the next page, thus providing him with
knowledge of results.

SUMMARY

We have seen that in the field of teaching machines
there is a dichotomy of opinion with respect to response
mode, step size, amount of error desirable, learning
theory, views on intelligence, and the supplementing of
traditional instructional methods. What we need now are
a lot of good experimental studies, both theoretical and
applied in nature

REFERENCES

ANGELL, G. W., Effect of immediate knowledge of quiz re-
    sults on final examination scores in freshman chemistry,
    J. educ. Res., 1949, **42**, 391-394.

BESNARD, G. G., BRIGGS, L. J., and WALKER, E. S. *The im-
    proved subject matter trainer*. Technical memorandum, Arma-
    ment Systems Personnel Research Laboratory, Lowry Air
    Force Base, Colorado, April 1955.

BRIGGS, L. J., The development and appraisal of special pro-
    cedures for superior students and an analysis of the effects of
    "knowledge of results." *Abstr. Doctoral Disser.*, 1949, **58**,
    482.

CROWDER, N. A. *An automatic tutoring book on number sys-
    tems*. Vol. 1. Timonium Md.: Electronics Co., 1958.

FERSTER, C. B., and SAPON, S. N., An application of recent
    developments in psychology to the teaching of German,
    Harvard educ. Rev., 1958, **29**, 23-27.

GLASER, R., DAMRIN, D. E., and GARDNER, F. M., The tab item: a technique for the measurement of proficiency in diagnostic problem solving tasks, *Educ. psychol. Measmt,* 1954, **14**, 283-293.

HOLLAND, J. G., A teaching machine program in psychology and its classroom use. Paper presented at Conference on Teaching Machines, Univer. of Penna., December 1958.

HOMME, L., and GLASER, R., Relationships between the programmed textbook and teaching machines. Paper presented at Conference on Teaching Machines, Univer. of Penna., December 1958.

PORTER, D., Some effects of year-long teaching machine instruction in an elementary school. Paper presented at Conference on Teaching Machines. Univer. of Penna., December 1958.

PRESSEY, S. L., A simple device for teaching, testing and research in learning, *Sch. & Soc.,* 1926, **12**, 373-376.

————, Development and appraisal of devices providing immediate automatic scoring of objective tests and concomitant self-instruction, *J. Psychol.,* 1950, **29**, 417-447.

SKINNER, B. F., Teaching machines, *Science,* 1958, **128**, 969-977.

Part II

EDITOR'S NOTE

Three approaches to programming have been developed; because of limitations of space only that used most frequently is represented in this collection of readings. In David Klaus' article which follows only linear *programming utilizing a* constructed-response *format is discussed in detail. This has been called the Skinnerian type of program. The second approach is called "intrinsic programming" or branching and it usually is identified with Norman Crowder (1959). In this technique, the student is given a unit of information containing a question or a problem followed by a set of multiple-choice answers from which he selects one. If his choice is correct, the student continues on to the next unit of information, if his choice is incorrect, he is instructed to go to a sub-program (in a scrambled book, to a page) which explains his error to him and instructs him to try the same or a similar problem again. The third approach combines the linear or sequential technique and the branching technique by instructing the student to skip a set number of frames if his solution to a problem is correct. The difference between the Crowder and the Skinner approaches is not mere mechanics—It involves a distinct difference in philosophy of teaching. A thorough discussion of these approaches to programming may be found in Rigney and Fry (1961).*

7

The Art of Auto-Instructional Programming

DAVID J. KLAUS*

American Institute for Research

With the possible exception of large-scale group testing, no one development in the field of psychology seems to have as much potential for the better utilization of human resources as auto-instructional methods. The technique has promise for producing a genuine and large scale improvement in educational practices and, as a consequence, it is expected to have a tremendous impact on the quality of classroom instruction. Because of the novelty of the technique and its potential impact on education, it is not at all surprising that auto-instruction is more frequently talked about than understood, and that more predictions are made as to its potentials than facts are collected as to its capabilities.

Perhaps more than anyone else, the professional educator should keep himself well informed as to where auto-instruction has been and where it is going. He should know not only the facts and the forecasts, but since he has the responsibility for wisely using these

* This article is based on a paper read at the Seminar on Educational Research at Cornell University in December 1960. This paper originally appeared in *Audio Visual Communication Review*, 1961, 9, 130-142, and it is reprinted here with the permission of the author.

materials, it is especially important that he become acquainted with the art of programming—the preparation of auto-instructional programs.

Sooner or later, educators and teachers are going to have full responsibility for writing programmed materials for classroom use, but unfortunately, programming is still a skill about which we know very little. The rules we have are incomplete at best, and for this reason, perhaps the greatest need at this moment is for a clarification of the techniques involved in preparing auto-instructional materials. Efforts along these lines will not only facilitate increased research and development, but will permit the preparation and rapid utilization of a large number of programs in our schools. But before illustrating what appear to be important characteristics of good as opposed to poor programs, it may be helpful to describe a little about what programming is, where it has been, and where it may be headed.

In essence, the auto-instructional method promotes the orderly and controlled development of an individual's skill in much the same way as a good tutor might do. By presenting lessons in small, carefully sequenced steps, complicated skills can be developed by gradually progressing from very simple to very complex levels of performance. Since the student must perform actively at each step during training, it is possible to carefully guide the development of his skill by means of immediate confirmation as to the correctness of each response. Furthermore, the auto-instructional technique facilitates the evaluation and improvement of the materials during the course of their development in that the difficulty level or contribution of each step can be carefully ascertained and, when necessary, any step may be modified or revised.

In Fig. 1 three frames from physics are used to illustrate how programmed materials of the kind we have been preparing at the American Institute for Research appear to the student. As illustrated in Frame 1, the student is exposed to material in the form of a small step which is designed in such a way as to encourage him to respond. Before beginning the program, the student is told to respond while he reads through the frame.

In general, he is to write his answers either directly in the book where the frame appears, on a separate answer pad, or if an auto-instructional device or "teaching machine" is used, on a strip of paper. As soon as he has completed the three responses called for, the student can expose the correct answers either by turning a page or advancing the machine. There, the student would see the three answers, *heat*, *energy*, and *heat*, which he can check against the responses he had given. Then, the

Frame 1	A fire can keep us warm because it gives off energy in the form of .... The sun also gives off .... in the form of ....
Frame 2	Heat is one form of .... Physicists call it thermal energy. A quart of boiling water has more .... energy than a quart of cold water.
Frame 3	As a warm object grows cooler, it loses heat, that is, it loses .... energy. When a cool object gets warmer, it gains ...., that is, it gains* ....

* The asterisk indicates that more than one word belongs in that space.

Fig. 1. Three frames from a program in physics.

student would again turn the page or advance the program and look at the second frame, shown in Frame 2.

The student again would respond and then check to see if his answers are correct. He would then turn to the third frame, shown in Frame 3. Learning that heat is energy, or more specifically, thermal energy, is not very astonishing in itself. But in terms of a high school physics program of 15,000 or 16,000 frames, it can be seen how each small step gradually and systematically produces a substantial amount of learning.

Research already accomplished indicates in a general way what can be achieved by means of auto-instructional programs. Under the sponsorship of the Office of Education, Dr. Lumsdaine and I prepared six weeks of high school physics in auto-instructional form. From these studies we were able to conclude that when used as a supplement to an otherwise full program of instruction, programmed materials do add significantly to student achievement. Furthermore, the evidence we obtained also suggested that auto-instructional programs may be relied upon to provide instruction, in physics at least, independent of classroom lectures and recitation.

The use of auto-instructional programs has not been limited, of course, to developing proficiency with the facts and concepts of physics. Holland and Skinner at Harvard University have prepared a considerable portion of the introductory psychology course in programmed form. Glaser and his associates at Teaching Machines, Incorporated have prepared a program to teach descriptive and inferential statistics at the college level, and Eigen and Komoski[1] at Collegiate School have prepared a program to teach logic to children at the elementary school level.

Industrial organizations have also begun to explore the value of auto-instructional materials for their technical training programs. We recently assisted a group of psychologists and instructors at IBM as they began the preparation of programs to teach the operation and maintenance of equipment as well as the programming of giant computers. At HumRRO in Washington, Rocklyn has prepared a program which provides instruction in oral Russian which can be used, despite the limited vocabulary involved, to deal with Russian speaking individuals; Shettel and Angell at the American Institute for Research have prepared a program to teach certain perceptual skills involved in the operation of a SAGE center to Air Force trainees; and Audrey Holland has prepared a program at the University of Pittsburgh to provide preliminary corrective ear training to students with articulatory speech defects.

We now have reason to believe that even higher order skills than these can be taught by means of auto-instruc-

---

[1] Mr. Komoski has been named president of the newly established Center for Programed Instruction, 365 West End Avenue, New York, N.Y.

tion. We are currently engaged in an investigation of methods for teaching art judgment. While the program being prepared will include some information on art history and principles, it has as its major purpose the development of a feeling of appreciation for art and the ability to differentiate good art from that which is not. We are also attempting to develop a program to provide laboratory instruction in electronics which will involve the use of actual laboratory equipment and a program to instill in students the insight necessary to solve geometric theorems which they have never before seen.

The success we have achieved thus far in broadening the applications of auto-instructional programs has led many of us to a feeling of cautious enthusiasm with respect to the progress that has been made. As more research is completed and more programs developed, we should have a still better understanding of the role that auto-instructional methods might have in the classroom of the future. The research that will contribute toward this goal must be carefully done. One of the most encouraging characteristics of auto-instructional materials is that they almost uniformly are capable of providing individual instruction, no matter how well or how poorly the program is written. All programs are not, and most certainly will not be, of equal quality. Until more objective and empirical measures of auto-instructional effectiveness become available, the educator must be adequately sophisticated in his judgment to evaluate the teaching competence of a program he might use in the classroom.

The educator must also be aware of the pitfalls in doing research on auto-instructional technology, both with regard to his own work and to evaluating experiments by others. The results of a study which depends on a poorly written program should be interpreted accordingly. Programming is at least as much of an art, at the current time, as clinical psychology, for example. No matter how fine an experimenter one is, he is not in a position to evaluate clinical patients using a Rorschach or base a study on his interpretation of projective test protocols unless he has been thoroughly trained in clinical techniques. Similarly, despite how well the experiment has been designed, its implications for a science of programming are limited if the program writers have not had sufficient experience. This is especially true when the sequence of frames is very small. A surprising number of studies have been carried out using a "program" only 50 or 60 frames long. The validity of the conclusions drawn from such experiments should be strongly questioned.

PROGRAMMING STEPS

Now to return to the problem of how programs are written. Because it is the area with which I am most familiar, I will describe the procedures we have been using to program physics at the American Institute for Research. It should be noted, though, that the technique for preparing programs varies from individual to individual and, furthermore, that it is frequently modified because of the nature of the subject matter involved.

Our first step is to list with care the specific objectives we will attempt to achieve with the program, expressed in clear, behavioral terms. Most often, these objectives represent criterion behaviors, that is, the particular responses we would like to see in the student's repertoire when he completes the program. For academic material, criterion behaviors often can be expressed in terms of a comprehensive test covering the entire course.

It is at this point that we make some initial decisions as to what kind of program will be constructed. For example, if the test (and the goal which it represents) requires only the ability to recognize the correct alternative as on a multiple-choice test, the programmer will attempt to achieve only this goal. It is not necessary, then, for him to prepare frames requiring constructed responses similar to those in the preceding figures. In the same way, if the student is required to know how to use a particular formula but not remember it, the programmer will plan to teach him just that, and no more. It has been our experience that, for academic subjects at least, the educational goal usually is to provide the student with the skills necessary to recognize a given principle when he comes across it, express the principle using his own words, and apply the principle to a new situation or problem. Typical criterion behaviors which might be listed for a unit on heat, for example, might include such questions as: What is heat? How is it measured? What is the principle of linear expansion? Show how Boyle's law might be applied, and so forth.

Once the objectives have been identified, the next step is to carefully prepare a course outline covering the material that we wish to teach. The outline is frequently derived from a number of textbooks, reference sources, and from the comments of teachers familiar with the subject matter area. In addition, we have found that it has been highly desirable for us to obtain the assistance of a technical expert in the subject matter field. This expert is given the task of reviewing the materials prepared at each phase of the program's development and is indispensable in preventing the dissemination of errors. We have also found that a well-qualified expert frequently can supply a large number of specific examples and interesting illustrations which can be incorporated into the program.

The third step in our procedure is to begin the preparation of draft frames. One of our programmers is assigned to each major unit and he or she is responsible for drafting groups of frames which cover the subject matter contained in the outline in such a way as to achieve the behavioral objectives of the course. We find that the process of drafting frames often points to inadequacies in the outline. Breaking down material into very small steps frequently identifies not only omissions in the outline but instances where it contains material which does not reflect the course objectives.

The draft frames are then edited three times. The first editing is done by another programmer who attempts to simplify the program and discover errors which the original programmer has made. The second editing is done by the technical expert who reviews the frames to insure their technical accuracy. A third editing is done by someone skilled in writing. Frames, just like textbooks, can either be interesting or dull. Our third editor reviews frames, rewording those that are awkward or unclear and revising others so that the program is enjoyable to work with as well as instructional.

At this point, the most important step in the preparation of a program is begun. The frames are shown to a trial subject who proceeds through the program as a student might eventually do in a classroom. Each answer is carefully recorded and, on the basis of the data obtained, the program is revised as much as necessary by either adding new frames or rewording those already in the program. It is at this step, possibly, that the difference between auto-instructional techniques and what many teachers do in the classroom is most pronounced. In programming, we assume that the burden of instruction rests with the program and not with the learner. Thus, when the student makes an error, it is assumed to be the fault of the program and not some inability on the part of the trial subject.

When the frames are revised, the trial procedure is repeated. In fact, 10 or 15 trial subjects are often used in the preparation of a single sequence of frames. The programmer is rarely satisfied that his materials are as good as they can be until trial students not only show that they have mastered the material in terms of how well they do on the criterion tests, but can proceed through the program without making an error. Following the last revision of the program, the frames are again reviewed by the technical expert and only then are they reproduced for field tryout.

The most difficult step in this procedure is the actual writing of the frames. As I noted earlier, we have barely begun to understand what makes a good frame. We do have a number of leads, however, that can be derived from laboratory studies of animal learning. I have discovered that educators often have a particular aversion to discussing the problems of classroom education in terms of how animals learn in the laboratory, but watching a rat, pigeon, or a chimpanzee learn can be a very instructive experience. The laboratory animal is not burdened with problems of low aptitude, inadequate readiness, lack of interest, or an unfortunate home life. Instead, the experimenter accepts the animal as is and modifies his own behavior to the extent necessary to produce learning.

The aspect of animal learning with particular importance for preparation of an auto-instructional program is the methods used for initially generating the correct response. Not only are these methods important with respect to auto-instruction, but perhaps one of the prime objectives of research in education today is the discovery of techniques for getting appropriate responses to occur initially. Probably this is our most ineffective skill in education and training. In teaching swimming, for instance, it is often quite difficult to get the correct response to occur the first time. The same is perhaps equally true of physics or spelling. The fewer similar or equivalent responses the student has, the less likely the responses are to occur at the appropriate time in the training schedule for practicing and reinforcement.

In the laboratory, we often wait until the animal makes a response before reinforcing him. We have found, though, that it is not necessary for the animal to make a complete response, but only make responses which are preparatory or similar to the desired response. If we reward these preparatory responses, a procedure called successive approximations, we speed training since the animal is taught behaviors which make the criterion behavior more likely.

Another procedure is to control the environment in such a way as to prevent erroneous responses from occurring. For instance, we can reduce the size of the apparatus until almost the only response that the animal can make is the desired one. The third possibility is to build on the animal's previous learning. We can teach a rat to run through a complicated maze quite readily if we first train the animal to follow lights and then place the lights appropriately in the proper alleys of the maze. By and large, these procedures are not systematically employed in education. For example, while we try to limit the environment in the laboratory, teachers are often encouraged to decorate their classrooms and provide other stimulation which, in fact, produce unwanted responses rather than eliminating them. I have always been struck by the amount of time a teacher spends in carefully decorating her room and the subsequent difficulty she has in maintaining the attention of students who are attracted to the displays she has put up.

Despite the rather obvious implications these laboratory studies have for improving instruction, a surprising number of programs have been constructed on the philosophy that the student is bound to make errors while learning. These programs typically incorporate a feature which is called branching, that is, alternate sequences to be used by the student after he has made an error. The same philosophy leads to the construction of devices which are capable of preventing cheating. One wonders, though, whether branching or cheating must be a problem in education. After all, since we want the student to practice being right, why not help him as much as we can? In preparing auto-instructional materials, then, the programmer generally makes every effort to carefully guide the student through the required learning. He designs the program so that it plays an active role in insuring that learning will take place and that the proper responses will be those that are practiced.

This particular approach to learning, which depends largely on placing the pupil in a carefully controlled environment, is not necessarily alien to education. Credit for the suggestion that instruction might be automated by properly arranging the circumstances in the student's environment is often given to Socrates or Pressey or Skinner. It is my own feeling, though, that many of our current notions on auto-instruction were accurately anticipated by John Dewey. To him, learning came about by doing; not random doing, however, but doing under such careful control that the student would necessarily meet with success when he was exposed to the consequences of his actions. Controlled or guided practice which leads to reward is the central theme in both Dewey's approach and that used in auto-instruction.

PROGRAMMING RULES

Now, let us look at some of the rules we have for building frames. While these rules generally represent the theory of auto-instructional programming rather than experimental evidence, they illustrate the auto-instructional method and thus might be a help at this time. The first is, that the student learns from making a response and not from hearing or seeing it. Only by practicing a response will a student learn and retain it.

In programming, the question often arises as to whether it is important that the student make his response overtly or whether it is sufficient for him to make a covert response. With respect to simple verbal material, there appears to be no difference produced by these methods. On the other hand, if the goal of the program is to develop some manual or perceptual skill, active responding seems to be very important. The same is true when the student is apt to over estimate the ease with which he learns. Only when the student writes out a new and unfamiliar word does he receive the necessary practice in spelling it. Pronouncing the word to himself will not likely yield as satisfactory a result.

Another question that often arises is whether to require multiple-choice or constructed responses. Since they are capable of doing so, programs can and should encourage the student to express his ideas in his own words. We then are sure that the student's practice is of the kind we usually want to generate; by means of constructed responses we require the student to use and explain what he knows so that he practices presenting his ideas and his knowledge instead of simply recognizing a correct answer from among the alternatives given. There is still one more advantage to have overt, recorded responses. This is to provide the programmer with the data necessary for further revision of his program. The first rule of programming: *require active responding*.

The next concern of the programmer is how to insure that the student will make a correct response, especially the first time that particular response is required. Aside from the laboratory methods described earlier, the programmer can get assistance in this matter by studying the techniques used in advertising. In most instances, the advertiser is primarily concerned with producing the initial response. Some of the more effective advertising we have is based on the contiguity learning principles of Guthrie and Estes. Their theories suggest that a given response can be readily produced providing we mass sufficient cues and present them all at the same time. When driving down the highway, a motorist is apt to come to an intersection where his stopping is made rather certain due to the presence of a stop sign, a flashing red light, and appropriate yellow lettering on the pavement.

In programming, each frame must contain sufficient cues to produce the desired response. Sometimes we can get the proper response to occur by the use of wording; at other times, we may use rhyming, synonyms, or particular word patterns we can assume are already in the repertoire of the students involved.

Appropriate cueing is one of the essential characteristics of a good frame. In fact, this is the essential difference between a test question and an auto-instructional frame. In giving a test, we design the items in it to at least partially lead the student astray. We don't want every student to get every answer correct. In a well-constructed program, however, every effort is made to insure that every student gets every response correct. The second rule: *proper cueing*.

The fact that a student can make a correct response is rarely of interest to us unless the response is made in the appropriate context. Little Johnny may be doing an excellent job of pronouncing "daddy," but after the first few times we hear it, we fail to think much of this response unless it occurs in the presence of the proper man. As learning proceeds during the course of using an auto-instructional program, the student must be gradually weaned from the liberal cues we have supplied, so that he can make the correct response without our help in the presence of the relevant context. Third rule for writing a good frame: *appropriate context*.

Together, these first three rules can be combined to describe a good frame. Basically, a good frame consists of only four parts. First is the response, selected beforehand. This is the part of the frame that must be left blank. Too frequently, a beginning programmer finds that even though he has selected a satisfactory response, he constructs the frame in such a way that some irrelevant word rather than the desired response is practiced. The second portion of a good frame contains whatever cues are necessary to reliably produce the desired response. Neither overcueing nor undercueing is desirable. The third characteristic of a good frame is that it contains some relevant context, that is, the kind of stimuli we hope will be capable of evoking the desired response at some time in the future. Early in the program, context will probably be at a minimum and cueing will be quite prevalent. By the end of the program, however, cueing should have vanished so that the appropriate responses are made solely in the presence of the appropriate context. The fourth ingredient of a frame is optional. We call it enrichment. We have found that, in many instances interest in a program is heightened by inserting facts such as names or dates which are relevant to the material being covered but not part of the course objectives. Aside from these four ingredients, everything else in a frame is superfluous.

The next characteristic of a good program is that it proceeds in very small steps. This is a rather difficult point to get across to a new programmer. Several studies have indicated, however, that the more steps, the better. In fact, the data seemed to indicate that a student proceeds faster through a program purposely made longer by the division of frames into smaller units than he does through a very condensed program. The number of frames in a program is not necessarily a good index of its efficiency, but as is the case in many other areas, one seems to get what one pays for, that is, the more frames the better. Rule four: *small steps*.

As the program is developed, the role of careful sequencing becomes evident. Most subject matter consists of material of unequal difficulty. Complex concepts are built on simple concepts. Long involved formulae often can be shown to represent several shorter formulae combined together. In preparing a program, the writer can greatly enhance its efficiency by thoroughly determining beforehand what the sequence of topics will be. The fifth rule of programming: *careful sequencing*.

Another problem having to do with the program as a whole is the problem of how often and how frequently a response should be practiced. As was the case with the number of steps, the rule here seems to be that the greater the number of repetitions, the better. The repeated review of a given response is almost universally more irritating to the programmer than it is to the learner. In the first place, the program writer already knows the response. To him, frequent repetitions are terribly tedious. From the student's point of view, however, repetitions can be terribly important. It is one of the basic principles of learning that retention of a response depends quite heavily on the amount of overlearning that has taken place. Thus, when a student complains of having made a certain response too often, we should be careful not to delete so much practice with that response as to affect its retention.

One guide to assure that repetition is frequent enough is that the programmer, in reviewing his own frames, should be sensitive to his echoic behavior. When a particular response stops ringing in his ears, it is probably time to review that response in the program. It is probably helpful, in addition, to introduce as much variation as possible in the cueing and context associated with a particular response each time it is repeated. This kind of variability can be expected to reduce monotony and also to induce a desirable amount of generalization with respect to that response. The sixth rule for programming: *frequent repetition.*

The next rule concerns the technical accuracy of the material contained within the program. The preparation of an auto-instructional program is a great amount of work. Too often, a writer engages in the necessary effort but fails to realize that the very excellence of his program in a psychological sense insures that his students will learn well, but learn the wrong facts and concepts. Insuring technical accuracy, of course, also involves the inclusion and exclusion of material. It is often the case that a programmer attempts to include too much into his program to permit the proper coverage of any one topic. In general, it is probably more advisable to do a thorough job on somewhat less material than an incomplete job on a larger amount. The seventh rule: *knowledge of the subject matter.*

Now we come to a few don'ts. Probably the most common mistake made by a beginning programmer is that he prepares the frames as if he were a lecturer presenting information.

The lecturer can be contrasted with the tutor or auto-instructional program in that he guides the student in what to learn but then delegates to the student the responsibility for structuring the material in small steps, for sequencing these steps, for scheduling sufficient practice, and for meeting with the success that will serve to reward desirable responses. Imitating a lecturer, the inexperienced programmer writes a paragraph for the student to read and follows it with a question which the student is expected to answer. Frame A shown in Fig. 2 is an example of this type.

Frame A	Temperature and heat have different meanings. Heat, the amount of thermal energy stored in an object, depends on the mass of the object and what it is made of as well as its temperature. Heat is measured in calories, but since heat and temperature are not the same, we do not measure .... in calories.
Frame B	In general, liquids, solids, and gases will expand when heated. Kerosene is a ....; it will expand when heated.
Frame C	Most metals contract when they solidify, but there are exceptions to this rule. For example, bismuth and antimony do .... contract when they go from a liquid to a solid state.
Frame D	Copper, iron, wax, and glass all contract when they solidify. Most substances, in fact, ... when they go from a liquid to a solid state.
Frame E	An astronomer, Anders Celsius, invented the centigrade scale of temperature. A thermometer which reads 100 degrees in boiling water is measuring the temperature of the water according to the .... scale of temperature.
Frame F	The centigrade scale of temperature is more properly called the .... scale, after the name of its inventor.

Fig. 2. Six frames illustrating weaknesses and stratagems in programming.

Programmers lecture in frames when they are not sure what they want to teach, when they have not clearly identified the specific objectives of the frame. Analyzing this frame in terms of cue, context, and response, we see that it is quite possible that a student could answer the frame solely on the basis of the last sentence. The other material in the frame, representing facts which the programmer might want the student to know, neither helps produce the response called for nor does it provide the kind of context in which we want the response of temperature to necessarily occur. In programming, we not only provide facts to the learner, but we help him to learn. If the student doesn't understand, it is our fault, not his. This is the eighth rule of programming: *don't lecture, teach*.

Frame B illustrates another very common error made by beginning programmers. Here the programmer had the beginnings of a quite satisfactory frame, but after he had written out a statement, he then selected a rather trivial word to be filled in by the student. The frame could be improved tremendously had he left the word "liquid" where the blank is now and removed the word "expand." It is the concept of expansion, after all, which the programmer was apparently attempting to teach. Advanced programmers sometimes make almost an opposite error. They decide that because the word or response itself seems trivial, it is not important enough to be left blank.

Frame C illustrates a frame that calls for such a response. Here, the word "not" *is* important. The fact that bismuth and antimony do *not* contract is the point we are trying to get across. The ninth rule of programming: *evoke a relevant response*.

Frame D illustrates another one of the rules. It illustrates how we can frequently depend on rather subtle cues to insure that the appropriate response will occur. It was not necessary, in this instance, to tell the student previously that most substances contract when they solidify. Instead, we have let the student make his own generalization and discover his own principle. The tenth rule: *don't provide more cues than necessary*.

Now look at the next frame (Frame E) in Fig. 2.

This frame, while not especially well written, does get its point across but it also illustrates another important error. The programmer may have assumed that his students would recognize the relationship between 100 degrees, boiling water, and the centigrade scale of temperature. I suspect that if we tried this frame on a large number of students, we would find that several of them would make the error of inserting the word Fahrenheit (if they could spell it) into the blank. This is our eleventh rule: *don't assume too much knowledge.*

In the last frame in Fig. 2 (Frame F), we can see that the author failed to recognize that we learn from responding and not from reading. It is very unlikely that the response *Celsius* would be evoked here in the average student unless he had previously learned the astronomer's name. Recalling the preceding frame, we can see one possible source for the programmer's error. He attempted to present too many facts within a single frame. The twelfth rule is: *don't present two new facts in one frame.*

These twelve rules sum up much of what we know about the art of programming at this time. As noted earlier, they tend to be incomplete, and we have not yet achieved our objective of being able to provide firm directions to beginning programmers. The lack of definitive rules, however, does encourage many programmers to experiment and thereby produce new rules and new concepts of programming. Perhaps one of the greatest errors that a programmer can make is attempting to copy the kinds of programs he has seen before. His objectives will frequently be too minimal, his program uninteresting, and he will fail to produce the kind of learning that he feels should occur in the classroom. There is no reason, for instance, why the blank in a program shouldn't represent a sentence or two. As another example, there is no reason why the programmer can't employ pictures —or for that matter, even have the students draw their own. We have used both of these kinds of responses in our physics program.

The last two frames I would like to illustrate both represent instances where the student is required, in terms of the way the frame is structured, to create a response which he may never have seen before.

The first frame in Fig. 3 (Frame G) is an example of this type. Here the word "also" cues the response. The student may never have seen the word "Kelvin" before, but yet he is able to respond that Kelvin is a scale of temperature. This frame also illustrates the use of the instructional approach which I have been describing. In programming, the primary objective of each frame should be the active participation, of the student in terms of carefully guided or controlled practice. An auto-instructional program should not attempt to explain a principle to a student. Instead it should carefully lead him, one step at a time, toward the desired level of proficiency. Here, in this frame, we have done more than could be accomplished by presenting the fact that "Kelvin is a scale of temperature" to a student; we have forced him to actually practice the correct response, in the proper context, with a minimum of cues.

| Frame G | Centigrade and Fahrenheit are both scales of temperature. Kelvin is also a* .... |
| Frame H | Knowing that most metals expand when heated, and remembering that the period of a pendulum depends on the length of the rod, we would expect that a pendulum clock would .... time on a cold day. |

* More than one word belongs in this space.

Fig. 3. Two frames that lead to discovery by the student.

The next frame (Frame H) illustrates further the non-rote quality of learning possible to achieve with an auto-instructional program. In a frame of this sort, which ordinarily would have been preceded by steps which taught the two facts appearing in the first part of the frame, the student is encouraged to discover some new fact about the world around him. In neither this nor the preceding frame do we depend on explanations. Instead, we have tried, subtly, to guide the student and help him experience the satisfaction of being right, all on his own.

One of the greatest contributions which programming is likely to make to education is the clear realization and understanding of the learning and instructional processes. I suspect that concepts such as the careful control of responding to insure its initial accuracy may improve classroom teaching whether or not auto-instructional programs have been devised.

What I am saying is that the means for placing materials on paper is not as important as our understanding of the instructional process. To illustrate, not too long ago I read somewhere of a technique used at a school where every effort was being made to teach the children cooperation as opposed to competition. While this only represents one small part of the training that would likely be necessary, I feel it was an ingenious solution to provide the children in the pre-school playground with an assortment of toys of the kind that required the cooperative activity of two or more children. That is, teeter-toters instead of swings, and wagons so large that the strength of two children was required to move one. This example of programmed learning of a social skill or habit illustrates the point that while it may not always be feasible, practical, or economical to provide instruction independent of a human teacher, there seems no reason to believe that if a skill, fact, or concept can be taught, it would not be possible to achieve it using auto-instructional methods.

REFERENCES

CROWDER, N. A., Intrinsically programmed teaching devices, *Proceedings* of the Invitational Conference on Testing Problems. Princeton, N.J.: Educational Testing Service, 1959, 40-52.

RIGNEY, J. W., and FRY, E. B. A *Survey and Analysis of Current Teaching-Machine Programs and Programming.* Office of Naval Research, Contract Non r-228(22), Technical Report No. 31, 1961. (This article will be published as a supplement to *Audio-Visual Communication Review,* 1961.)

Part III

EDITOR'S NOTE

Predictably, the first studies of programmed instruction tended to be evaluative; i.e., the purpose of the studies was to compare programmed materials and conventional instruction on their efficiency as teaching devices. Quite predictably, for the majority of such studies, "no significant differences" was the conclusion. Once that it had been determined that programmed materials could teach, attention was directed toward research which would isolate some of the parameters of learning with material of this type. Only a relatively small amount of data is available at the time of writing, but it is sufficient to point the directions which research will take in the immediate future. Some of the areas for which more information is needed are:

What are the (1) characteristics of the "ideal" frame or step? This can be subdivided into (a) What are the characteristics of the "ideal" stimulus elements? (b) What are the characteristics of the "ideal" response element? (c) What type of confirmation technique is best? and (d) What type of activity will mediate best between the stimulus and response elements?

What type of programming technique results in the greatest gain, with time to learn held constant?

How well is knowledge acquired from programmed materials retained?

Is it necessary to develop programs which take individual differences in ability and motivation into consideration?

What type and quality of reinforcements should be used with programmed instruction?

What are the best criterion measures for evaluating learning from programmed materials?

What characteristics must a program have to insure satisfactory transfer of training?

What are the criteria needed to evaluate the quality of a program?

What learning models, if any, provide a satisfactory frame of reference for further developments in programmed instruction?

The articles which have been selected for Part III deal, in part, with the first five of the research problems listed above. The first five articles are concerned chiefly with knowledge of results as a confirming technique and the effects of the mode of response on learning. Two articles are concerned with the problem of individual differences and one with stimulus characteristics of the frame or step.

8

Development and Appraisal of Devices Providing Immediate Automatic Scoring of Objective Tests and Concomitant Self-Instruction*

S. L. PRESSEY
Ohio State University

A. "SELF-SCORING" TESTS: THEIR UNIQUE CONVENIENCE, AND USEFULNESS IN INSTRUCTION

The grading of conventional essay-type examinations has long been recognized as burdensome and slow. By contrast, the scoring of objective tests has seemed easy and prompt. But actually this latter task is by no means negligible, or as immediate as might be desired. Objective tests are most commonly multiple choice or true-false. The person taking the test checks the answers he considers right, on the test blank or on a separate answer sheet. The materials are then collected, and at some later time the errors are checked and counted. If test materials or simple testing devices could be developed such that,

---

* The work described in this paper was under subvention from the Special Devices Center of the Office of Naval Research, for development of devices for the facilitation of learning, working in cooperation with the Ohio State University Research Foundation, under the direction of the writer. This article is reprinted from *The Journal of Psychology*, 1950, **29**, 417-447, and is used here with the permission of the author and the editor.

*as a student answered each question, that answer was
immediately and automatically scored and recorded as
right or wrong,* then clearly much trouble would be saved.
Moreover, results would then *be available as soon as the
test was finished.* If a future emergency should necessitate the rapid training of large numbers of men, such
convenience and immediate availability of scores could
appreciably facilitate the training.

Additional advantages of self-scoring devices are more
important, however. A test in French or mathematics or
navigation is of little value if it does not in some way
further the student's learning of that subject. If he is
weak on certain points, the test should locate them and
aid in the remedying of these weaknesses. And this
should be done *promptly;* an instructor who never answers a student's question until 48 hours after it is asked
would be considered exasperatingly inefficient. The usual
testing methods are grossly at fault in all these respects.
Usually, the student does not find out how he did on a
test until a day or more after it was taken. Even then, he
may be given only his total score or grade, without any
indication as to questions missed. If the scored test
blanks are returned to him, he may be little or no better
off. Even if his errors have been marked on the test, he is
still left in ignorance as to which other answer on a multiple choice question is right. If separate answer slips are
used and these returned checked but without the test
blank, he knows for instance that he missed Questions 12
and 19 but does not know what Questions 12 and 19
were.[1] In contrast, self-scoring devices *inform the student
immediately, when he indicates his answer to an objective question, whether that answer is correct; if it is
wrong, he is at once automatically guided to the discovery
of the correct answer.* This quick incisiveness should substantially facilitate instruction. In an emergency, requir-

[1] The IBM electric test scorer is little better in the above
respects than hand scoring. Results are still not available until
a day or so after the test is taken. Some inspection of blanks
is often necessary to be sure that students have marked each
answer space adequately and not marked more than one for
each question. Each blank must then be fed through the
machine and its total score written on it. And the scored
blank does not show in any way which questions were missed.

ing the rapid training of large numbers of people, such integration of testing and teaching into one episode should be especially helpful.

Devices or special materials which at once inform a student about the correctness of his answer to a question, and then lead him to the right answer clearly do more than test him; *they also teach him.* And they do this in ways so in accord with basic laboratory findings and theory regarding the nature of the learning process that they constitute, to an exceptional degree, an example of human engineering. Theories of learning recognize the paramount and obvious importance of the learner's knowing whether each response he makes is correct or not. Research has shown that such knowledge is most effective if obtained without delay. There are data to indicate that answers found to be wrong, but not corrected, tend to be repeated. Other things being equal, the response which has been made most often, and most recently, is most likely to be made again. The devices suggested above provide that the learner always is informed about the correctness of every answer to every question on a test. That information is given immediately. If a mistake is made, the learner is at once guided to the right answer. This is always his last or most recent answer before leaving the question; and if the test is repeated it is almost certain to be made most often. Somewhat as the automatic pilot on a plane adjusts the flight more quickly and completely than a human pilot could do, so such devices spot each learner's weaknesses and assure their correction more adequately and immediately than could any human instructor.

As an instructional device, the self-scoring test has certain further advantages. An objective test can cover many more questions in a given time than a written examination or quiz. The self-instructional objective test can similarly cover more ground than would be possible otherwise. In a given time, it can in effect give individualized instructions to every student in a class (searching out the misconceptions of each student and then correcting them) over more questions than a tutor could cover with one student. A well made objective test has a more carefully considered and exactly phrased right answer than an instructor is likely to give in class discussion; and the wrong answers are carefully chosen as the most common misconceptions or mistakes. The self-instructional procedure systematically presents these for consideration and then clearly checks them off as wrong. In short, these devices should make it possible to cover more ground in a given time than a teacher could *and* do it more adequately.

The purpose of the present paper is, briefly to (*a*) describe means by which tests may be made self-scoring and self-instructional, (*b*) investigate the way in which such devices work, and (*c*) determine their value in educational or training programs.

B. MATERIALS AND METHODS

1. The "Self-Scoring" Device

The total project has involved development or improvement of several different devices.[2] However, the data of the present paper were all obtained with the "punchboard." This is a very simple unit the size of a three by five card, about one-half inch thick. A center of quarter-inch ply-board has riveted, on either side, two thin sheets of pressboard. Between the outside sheet and the second sheet is sufficient space for a slip of paper to be inserted; between the second sheet of the pressboard and the ply-board center is a removable key sheet of pressboard. On each face of the punchboard are two columns each of four rows of one-eighth inch holes, the

[2] The basic idea involved in all of them goes back to work by the writer in 1915 and was embodied in a mechanism for use with objective tests in 1922 (Pressey, 1926). It is believed that this work had some influence in stimulating efforts of other psychologists along these lines. The present project aimed originally at the development and appraisal of devices improving on these mechanisms. However, pending availability of these new pieces of apparatus, it seemed desirable intensively to investigate the value of self-scoring procedures. The punchboard was therefore devised and used for this purpose. No claim is made to originality regarding the "punchboard" method, the general idea of which goes back at least 20 years. Recently Dr. Maurice Troyer (Angell & Troyer, 1948) has been experimenting with a similar scheme. Other devices for immediate self-scoring will be touched upon later.

rows of four holes being numbered from one to 30. However, the key sheet has holes only for the right answer on the particular test to be used.

Test questions are usually presented on a mimeographed sheet, but may be given orally, put on the blackboard, projected on a screen, or otherwise presented as convenient. The testee takes a test by simply punching with a pencil point through the paper slip in that hole which corresponds to what he thinks is the right answer. For instance, if for Question 1 of the test he thinks the second answer is right, he will punch his pencil through the paper appearing in the second hole of the first row. If he *is* right, his pencil goes through the paper and down into the hole in the key sheet. But if he is wrong, the pencil barely breaks the paper and then comes up against the key sheet. He thus knows that he is wrong and tries another hole in Row 1, thus proceeding until the pencil goes deep.

After he has gone through a test, he can glance back and see on what questions he made a mistake (where he punched more than one hole or has a small hole). This can be done either before or after the sheet is withdrawn from the punchboard; and either before or after, it is easy to count up the number of small holes to obtain the error score. A space at the top of the front plate of the punchboard gives room on the paper for the testee to write his name and other information as well as the error score.

The device is very simple to use. There is no possibility of changing an answer (a hole cannot be unpunched). The punched papers, once withdrawn, can be filed and are a convenient record for item analysis or other study. The keys are so planned that each can be turned over or turned end for end, and thus give four different patterns. Two or three different key cards thus can total enough variations in pattern so that learning a key seems very unlikely. In setting up a test, the procedure is to prepare the pattern of right answers to correspond with one of the ready-made keys, which have been carefully planned to distribute the right answers over the four possibilities. However, it is relatively easy to punch a new key if one is desired. For true-false or other two-choice tests, four columns can be used on one side. The back side of the punchboard, which is made exactly like the front side but numbered "2," either permits a second trial on the test to find improvement and give more practice, or provides a total of 60 multiple-choice items.

2. The "Self-Instructional" Tests

The tests used with the punchboard in the experimentation to be reported almost all consisted of four-choice[3] objective questions, of which samples will be given shortly. Tests which consisted of a series of statements to be appraised as true (by punching the first hole) or false (by punching the second) were compact and relatively easy to make, but seemed somewhat less effective for instruction. Tests of this same type but with a third category of "uncertain" (shown by punching the third hole in a row) were tried but were hard to make, since defensible differences of opinion as to best answer them often appeared. A variety of other judgment, applicational, and special types of items were tried extensively. Some were believed to have distinctive values for self-instructional testing. However, they presented difficulties of one sort or another, and will not be described here.

Much consideration was given to the problem of desirable length of tests. Early plans were for 100 questions. However, for instructional purposes, frequent short tests were found better than more occasional long ones. Instructional tests were found most effective if followed by

---

[3] Early experimentation was with five-choice questions. However, it appeared that the great majority of items simply did not have four wrong answers which were all statements of errors that students were likely to make and needed to be warned against, or were otherwise justifiable in an instructional test to be used as these devices required. Where the most important function served by a test is instructional, each alternative answer should make a real contribution to instruction. Each wrong answer should be one against which a warning is needed, or which elucidates the question in some way. No alternative answer should confuse the student or introduce ways of construing the question which are not educationally profitable to consider. Poor alternatives waste time both in taking the test and in discussion after, and might confuse the learner rather than help him.

discussion the same hour. Even with so short a task as a 30-item true-false test, several runs through it with the punchboard were often found to be needed, if a perfect score was to be reached. All these and other considerations put together led to the conclusion that a self-instructional test of only about 30 or 40 questions was better than any longer unit. Moreover, such short tests had obvious practical advantages. With a little careful planning, a test of 30 four-choice questions could be put on one side of a single long mimeograph sheet, or 30 true-false statements on one side of a short sheet, and almost any test of that many items on two sheets or two sides of one. In addition, the punchboard could be kept small. For use on the arm of the usual classroom chair, such compact convenience was a distinct asset.

Initial experimentation was with a great variety of subject-matter ranging from nonsense syllables, vocabularies in a foreign language, and glossaries of naval terms, to technical articles and chapters from books used in the Naval R.O.T.C. training program at the University, and series of tests covering the required reading in two courses in psychology. It was finally decided to concentrate on material of three types. Russian vocabulary was used as rôte matter more interesting and valuable than nonsense syllables, equally unfamiliar to almost everyone, and indicative of possible values of self-instructional tests in learning a foreign vocabulary. Hard English vocabulary items were used to represent tasks such as the learning of technical terms where the material was highly meaningful but (in contrast to the subject-matter of a course) without any organization or structure. And the subject matter of two psychology courses served as an example of material which was highly organized, and part of a systematic program of instruction. The following excerpts from certain of these tests will illustrate the simple directions used and some typical items. The psychology test excerpt includes two features found distinctly useful for review study after a test is taken: headings in the test to give it structure, and page references so that if a student misses a question and wishes to look it up, he can turn at once to the place in the reading where that topic is treated.

Russian Vocabulary Study Test

Directions: In each line find the English word meaning the same as the Russian word, and punch your pencil into the hole corresponding to that English word. If your pencil goes deep, you are right, and should go on to the next line. But if your pencil barely breaks the paper, you are wrong, and must try again—until you do find the right answer.

1. ZAPISKA: (*a*) plate; (*b*) expensive; (*c*) note; (*d*) bridge.

27. POTOM: (*a*) depth; (*b*) then; (*c*) paper; (*d*) word.

English Vocabulary Study Test

Directions: Following each word, find the phrase you think nearest in meaning to it, and punch your pencil into the hole on the punchboard corresponding to that answer. If your pencil goes deep, you have the right meaning. If it does not, try the phrase you think next most likely to be right. Continue until you find the right answer. Then study that word so that you will know its meaning, if you are tested on it again.

1. INTEGUMENT; (*a*) a completed whole; (*b*) a covering as the human skin; (*c*) moral soundness; (*d*) a factor, as in mathematics.

19. INIMICAL: (*a*) favorable; (*b*) unique; (*c*) influential; (*d*) hurtful.

Psychology Study Test Abilities

Directions: Punch the hole indicating what you think the best answer to each question; if wrong, try again.

Special Ability: 12. A person superior in art usually has (*a*) poor social adjustment; (*b*) a good general ability and background of special opportunities and motivation; (*c*) a highly special innate capacity; (*d*) lack of ability in other areas. 68-1.

Appraisal of Ability: 24. The general ability of a person from a non-English speaking home may best be estimated by a (*a*) personal interview; (*b*) Binet test; (*c*) performance test; (*d*) group intelligence test. 77-1.

For some of these tests, several forms were available, using different keys. For the two courses, sufficient variety in material was sought to give interest and also prevent a routine approach. Thus for one topic there were two four-choice tests, a true-false-uncertain judgment test, and an application test consisting of a series of paragraphs each presenting a practical situation or episode followed by questions as to ways of best dealing with such a situation. There were also various check tests to determine the effects of the practice tests, which will be described later as used.

3. Groups Experimented With

At the Ohio State University the first and second courses in elementary general psychology and the first course in educational psychology are taught in sections of about 35 students, mostly freshmen and sophomores. In a given quarter there may be a total of as many as 50 sections. Most of these are taught by part-time instructors in their third or fourth year of work for the doctorate. Each course is under the supervision of a senior staff member; there is a regular calendar, certain objective examinations are taken by all sections, and there are frequent staff meetings. These numerous sections, thus coordinated and systematically appraised, offered unusual opportunity for the extensive group experimentation desirable in this project. Further, it was possible in the course in educational psychology to make sweeping changes in methods and hours of meeting when needed for experimental purposes. Most of the data are from various of these sections. However, students in certain other courses, from a how-to-study laboratory for freshmen on probation to certain graduate seminars, took part in the total investigation at one time or another. In short, for the three quarters of the regular school year, the total number of cases, sections, and facilities for this investigation seemed exceptional.

C. RESULTS

In attempting to appraise the value of devices involving immediate automatic scoring and self-instruction the natural first step was to determine whether, in fact, taking a test by such means would at once bring about learning. A natural next step was to investigate whether such devices were of service in regular instructional or training programs. A desirable third step was to see whether self-scoring tests might be exceptionally useful with special groups or instructional plans. These issues will be taken up in order.[4]

1. *Immediate Outcomes of Use of the Punchboard*

As mentioned earlier, Russian vocabulary, hard English vocabulary, and subject matter in Psychology (as illustrative of respectively, rôte matter, meaningful but unorganized material, and material organized and meaningful) were chosen to show how the punchboard worked with matter of various types. Certain immediate outcomes of such use are now to be considered.

a. Effect of the punchboard on range of test scores. Ordinarily a person taking a multiple choice test checks, for each question, the answer he thinks right; and his total score is the number of questions answered correctly, or answered incorrectly. In interesting contrast, a self-scoring procedure such as the punchboard can measure degrees of ignorance *for each question.* For example, on a four-choice question a student could make no errors, or one, two, or three. On 30 questions, the total possible errors could range from zero to 90 as compared with zero to 30 for the same test taken in the usual fashion. A procedure which increases the range of scores three times should discriminate more widely between those students who had the subject-matter well learned and those who still were grossly ignorant or had many misconceptions to correct.

A very simple experiment suggested that this was so. One college class was given a hard English vocabulary test in the usual way; each student checked the answer to each question which he thought right, and the score was the number of questions wrong. Lowest number of errors was 18 and highest 28, or a range of 10. Then another similar class was given the same test using the punchboard. Lowest number of errors was 19 and highest 53, or a range of 34! It would surely seem that a range of 34 would discriminate good from poor students more agreeably than a range of 10, or less than a third as much. Similarly the range on a 30-question test in psy-

---

[4] Acknowledgments for work on various phases of the total study should be made to Dr. Viola Cassidy, Dr. Leslie Briggs, Mr. Daryl Severin, and other assistants.

chology was 8 for the usual method of testing, but 33 using the punchboard. A test of Russian vocabulary, given immediately after five minutes study of the 30-word Russian-English vocabulary list, showed less difference in range (20 as compared with 26) because the preceding study had made the test too easy.[5] But the difference is nevertheless there.

b. Effect of use of the punchboard on number of errors when a test is immediately repeated. If students take a test in the usual way and then at once take it again, they would be expected to make about as many errors the second time as the first. Table 1 shows that they do so. In fact, sometimes they do a little worse the second time, as a result perhaps of boredom and carelessness. The first two columns show that when a class took a 30-word Russian vocabulary test in the usual way (the students simply checking what they thought the right answer) and then were immediately given the same test again in the same way, the median number of errors increased from 7 to 8. But a class which took this same test twice using the punchboard, showed a drop from 12 to 8 errors. With meaningful material the learning with the punchboard was even greater: from 43 to 7 errors on the English vocabulary test and 18 to 2 on the psychology quiz (Table 1).

It seems clear that the students do show some immediate learning as a result of using the punchboard. Apparently they gain more with meaningful material, and least on matter of a rôte type such as the Russian. The great gain in the English vocabulary might be explained as due to the great initial difficulty of these terms plus their basic familiarity, making them easily learned, once the punchboard gave reminders as to their meaning.[6]

---

[5] For this same reason, initial error scores on the Russian test in Tables 1, 2, and 3 following are probably lower than they should be for comparison with the results in hard English vocabulary and Psychology. But important conclusions appear not thereby affected.

[6] Detailed analysis of the above and other similar results indicated that the punchboard brought improvement in two ways. When a right answer was at once hit upon, the first time through a test, the punchboard confirmed this choice as right. But this effect was not very important. It brought gains over

TABLE 1

*Learning from taking a test with the punchboard,
as shown by decrease in errors on second testing.*

Subject matter of tests:	Russian		English		Psychology	
Method of giving tests:	As Test	Punch-board	As Test	Punch-board	As Test	Punch-board
Median[a] number of errors						
On first test	7	12	22	42	11	18
On second test	8	8	23	6	11	2
Decrease in errors	−1	4	−1	36	0	16

[a] The median is the point below and above which there are equal numbers of cases. Classes averaged 31 students in size.

c. Effects of the punchboard as evidenced by a test different in type from the practice tests. The above results were obtained with immediate repetition of the same test. Conceivably, learning brought about by the punchboard might be highly specific—perhaps a mere memorizing of the test material, or the key. If this were true, a second test different from the practice material would show little gain. The following simple experiment offers evidence that the learning was not so limited, that there was instead a real gain in knowledge of the matter presented.

The multiple-choice Russian test used previously was first given a class, using the punchboard. Then a very different test, a recall test, was given. On this recall test, the Russian words were listed in a different order from that in which they appeared on the practice test, and a space was provided after each Russian word for the student to write its English meaning. This same recall test

what occurred simply with repetition of the test as a test, of only about 5 per cent. The big effect of the punchboard was in correction of errors. The punchboard brought immediate right answer on second trial for about 65 per cent of items wrong on the first testing.

was given also to another similar class, after the practice test had been taken simply as a test. However, the order of items was different. And the "direction" of the thinking was reversed. In the check test, a definition was presented and the student indicated which of four difficult English words fitted the definition. In contrast, the practice test presented the word and the student chose the correct one of four definitions. The Psychology check test differed from the practice test in an even more elaborate fashion. Ten questions on one general topic did not appear in any form on the practice sheet; 10 were paraphrased from questions on the practice test; the remaining 10 were repeated from the practice series but appeared in a different sequence on the test, intermixed with the paraphrased and new questions, and with the order of the wrong answers and position of the right answers changed. This scheme was used extensively later in this study. Its purpose was to obtain evidence regarding the spread of punchboard learning as affected by the degree of similarity, in phrasing and idea, between the practice and the check tests. Table 2 summarizes the results of these check tests, given immediately after the corresponding practice test had been taken with the punchboard.

Effects of the punchboard are here not so great or so clearcut as in Table 1; a repetition of exactly the same test would inevitably show more gain than check tests which vary from the instructional test. However, on the English and psychology the differences are substantial and (as indicated by the note to Table 2) distinct. Analysis of the four-point gain in psychology showed three on the "re-arranged repeat" items and one point on the paraphrased—an analysis here of little reliability but later to be further investigated.

d. Effects of several consecutive repetitions of a test using the punchboard. If once through a practice test with the punchboard does bring some learning, several times through should bring more. However, if students go through the same self-instructional test several times in succession, it is conceivable that they might tend to learn the key or pattern of right answers rather than the information conveyed in the test. Or at least, they might

TABLE 2

Learning from taking a test with the punchboard, as shown by number of errors on a second test different in form.

Subject matter of tests:	Russian		English		Psychology	
Method of giving first test:	As Test	Punch-board	As Test	Punch-board	As Test	Punch-board
Median number of errors on second test	19	17	9^a	2	10^a	6

[a] Only 5 per cent of the class taking the English practice test simply as a test, and 12 per cent of those so taking the psychology practice test, did as well as or better than the median of the punchboard group. Table 3 following shows further reduction of Russian recall test errors to 10 after 5 punchboard testings. This is additional evidence that the practice tests were causing a learning which was not confined to mere rote learning of the practice test series. Again, these classes averaged 30 students in size.

learn that information so much in one particular order and context that use in other setting would be handicapped. To check on these points, one class was given the same Russian vocabulary test practice test four times using the punchboard, and then a recall check test, all in one class hour. A similar class was then given a series of practice tests covering the same words but with the order of items and the key or pattern of right answers changed each time; again the punchboards were used but changed each time to fit the key for that particular test. And again at the end of the series the recall and test was given. Similar series were run with same and changed tests in English vocabulary and psychology except that the length of the hour permitted only three times through the practice series, and left no time for an end test in psychology. Table 3 shows the median number of errors on each practice test and in the Russian check test.

On the Russian, the changing practice tests seem actually to handicap the learning, in that the median number

of errors actually goes up on the second trial, and thereafter continues higher than on the tests in which the

TABLE 3

*Decrease in number of errors with repeated taking of a practice test
using the punchboard, and effects of changing the order of questions
and the pattern of right answers upon such decrease.*[a]

| | Russian Vocabulary Practice | | | English Practice | | | Psychology Practice | |
| | Test | Check | | Test | Check | | Test | |
	1 2 3 4 5	Test		1 2 3	Test		1 2 3	
Median No. of errors								
Same test	11 8 5 3	10		42 14 5	6		17 4 1	
Changed test	13 15 9 9 6	10		41 17 8	5		18 3 1	

[a] Numbers of cases for Russian groups were 49 and 28, for English 29 and 41, and for psychology 33 and 34. Error scores on end
tests are mistakes plus omissions. Five minutes study of the Russian vocabulary list preceded the practice tests.

order was unchanged. However, the check test shows no
difference, at the end of the practice series. On the English vocabulary and psychology, results for same and
changed practice material are practically the same.

A natural interpretation of the above results is that
with such rôte learning as of the Russian, there tends to
be some dependence on the arrangement of items. However, in proportion to the meaningfulness and integration
of the material, change or sameness of key makes no
difference; attention is on the subject-matter, and that is
what is learned. Apparently with none of these subject-
matters does repetition of the practice test with the same
key handicap learning. It is even conceivable that the
same test and key in successive reviews might help. For
example, in reviewing a book it is an aid that one can
each time find a topic on the same page with same context, and upsetting if a review is of a different edition

where all these details are different. The analogy is of course only very rough, but it does seem suggestive of value in review of the same test. Some value would seem especially likely if the test questions were in a logical order and perhaps grouped under headings, as suggested a few pages back. Anyhow, these findings are indeed pleasant, since they support the more convenient repetition of the same test for practice. They also thus warrant use of a specialized device, for facilitating repeated runs through a practice test, to be mentioned later.[7]

In short, the punchboard does indeed appear to further learning. It is probably more effective with meaningful than rôte matter. Repeated use seems to carry learning further; and some repetition of the same test does not seem to cause mere learning of a particular test key or other unfortunate effect. However, the results so far have been with brief and relatively simple tests and checks on outcomes, all within one class hour. The practical question now is whether these procedures would be effective with more substantial learning tasks, and over a period of time.

2. The Punchboard, in a College Course, as a Testing Aid Not Integrated with Teaching

The most simple but obviously inadequate way to use a device like the punchboard is as a convenience in testing but without any attempt to tie its instructional potentialities in with teaching methods. Such a situation might occur if its use were required of teachers without interesting them in it or indicating ways of using it to aid instruction. Two trials of what might be called perfunctory use were made.

a. Use of punchboard tests for review. In the large second-quarter course in general psychology, eight chapters of the textbook were covered between the first and second midterm examinations. To help students in re-

[7] Readers familiar with the methods of Thorndike and others in the study of the law of effect will recognize that repetition of a test using the punchboard involves the "retained situation," the problem being "retained" before the learner until the right answer is found. It would seem that such devices as the punchboard could be very useful in such research. Results of such theoretical investigation will be reported in a later paper.

viewing for the second examination, two 60-item review tests were constructed. The first consisted of 20 multiple-choice questions on the first two chapters, 20 on the second two, and 20 more which were the first 20 repeated but in a different order. This review test was given to four sections totaling 114 students during the class hour preceding the midterm examination. A second review test similarly covering the second four chapters was given to six other sections, totaling 182 students. On the day following, all sections were given an objective midterm examination, having 21 questions repeated or para-phrased from the first review test, 22 similarly from the second practice test, and 24 questions which were on the same eight chapters but unlike questions on either review test.

TABLE 4

Percentages correct, of mid-term questions covered in a review practice test using the punchboard, and of other questions not thus reviewed.

	Group A	Group B
Questions not in practice tests	76%	75%
Questions in practice test given Group A	85	69
Questions in practice test given Group B	70	79

Table 4 shows that on these new questions the two groups did practically the same, thus indicating that they were essentially equal in ability and accomplishment aside from any help the practice tests might have given. On the midterm questions which were repeated or para-phrased from the first practice test the group which had taken it did distinctly better; similarly, the second group did better on questions from the review test it took. The differences are not great, but are significant. Table 5 indicates that use of the punchboard reduced errors most on the repeated questions. But some gain appeared also on those which had been rephrased from the practice test to the midterm.

In the above experiment, no significant differences

appeared between questions which appeared once and twice on the practice test. Initial difficulty was found very important, however. Obviously, the punchboard could bring no more than 5 per cent improvement on a question so easy that 95 per cent of the students at once answered it correctly on the practice test. On most of the difficult items, the device caused large gains. However,

TABLE 5

Per cents of students getting questions right on midterm which they
(a) had taken on a practice test using the punchboard, and
(b) had not taken on a practice test.

	Not Taken in Practice Test	Taken With Punch- board	Gain From Punch- board Test
Questions paraphrased from practice test to midterm	69	72	3
Questions repeated from practice test to midterm	69	87	18

The table shows that 72 per cent of the students got questions right on the midterm which they had had in different wording on a practice test using the punchboard. However, only 69 per cent of students got these questions right if they had not taken them in the practice test. The punchboard practice test thus brought a gain of 3 per cent; in repeated questions the gain was 18 per cent.

on a few paraphrased questions, the practice test actually caused loss, presumably because of tricky rephrasing.

b. Value of frequent brief practice tests using the punchboard. In the next quarter, trial was made of the possible value of frequent brief testing using the punchboard, in the second month of the course in general psychology, in which eight chapters of the test were covered. Four 20-question practice tests were made up, each sampling points covered in two chapters. On the day when discussion of one of these two chapter units was to begin, five sections totaling 149 students took the practice test on that unit using the punchboard. Afterward, any questions about the test were answered; but since the instructors regarded the testing as an experiment in which they had no hand, they did not encourage discussion nor use the test in their plan of teaching. Five other sections, totaling 152 students, on the same days took these same practice tests in the usual fashion of test-taking; they simply marked on the test sheet what they thought to be the right answers. The papers were then collected, graded after class with all errors marked, and returned the next day. At this time the instructor went over the questions, indicating the right answers, and giving opportunity for discussion. This procedure might be considered to lean over backwards in the effort to assure full demonstration of the values of frequent test without the punchboard. A total of more class time was given to the tests than to the punchboard procedure. The tests were seen twice, on two different days. Probably in most classes in which frequent brief tests are given, the scored tests are returned less promptly, and without such review of questions and right answers. A third group of five sections covered the same ground, but without taking the practice tests in any way. Most of the instructors had two sections; and as far as possible it was arranged that each had one of one type and one of another.

Evidence as to the initial status of the three sets each of five sections before the experiment began was yielded by the first midterm examination, since all 15 sections used the same instructional procedure during this first month of the course. The first row of figures in Table 6, giving the average per cent of right answers made by each group on this first examination, shows the "no practice test" group initially best and the punchboard group poorest. On the second midterm the two groups which have taken the practice tests are slightly above the first group. Analysis shows the punchboard group best on the 25 questions repeated and 15 paraphrased from the practice tests, but poorest on new questions—as might be anticipated from their initial bottom position (Table 6).

Occasional brief tests not closely tied in with instructional methods thus brought only slight gains. Tests given in the ordinary way, scored after class, then returned and discussed the next day, were about as effective

TABLE 6

Percentages of questions answered correctly by three groups of students (a) on the first midterm, before the experiment began, (b) on the second midterm, and (c) on each type of question in the second midterm.[a]

	Groups of Students		
	No Practice Tests Taken	Tests Taken as Test	Tests Taken With Punch-board
First midterm	69	68	66
Second midterm	73	78	76
28 questions not in the practice tests in any form	73	75	69
15 paraphrased questions	77	82	83
25 repeated from practice tests	71	81	83

[a] Five sections in each group, the first totaling 149 students, the second 152, and the third 149.

as the punchboard. However, it did save the work of scoring, also the trouble and time of returning answer slips the next day and going over test questions and right answers with the class then. But it would seem that tests should not be merely occasional episodes incidental to the instruction, but rather be closely integrated with the instruction method. What might the gains then be?

3. Use of Practice Tests With the Punchboard as a Major Instructional Method, by the Instructor in Charge of the Class

This experimentation was in the course in educational psychology, which follows one in general psychology, is most commonly taken in the freshman year, is taught in sections of about 35 students, and meets five times a week for one class hour. For this work, a large number of practice tests had been carefully prepared, with special emphasis on problems of judgment and application.

a. Value of intensive use of punchboard tests as compared with carefully planned discussion by the same instructors. First, what might be accomplished by using the punchboard as a major instructional device, on certain units of the course? These units or topics (as, transfer of training) were in the course calendar allotted two or three class hours. On the first day assigned to such a unit, the experimental sections took a 30-item practice test using the punchboard, at the beginning of the hour. When a student finished the test, he looked up any doubtful questions, and discussed these with other students and the instructor. Since it was understood that the practice tests would not be used directly as a basis for grading, but rather as an aid toward preparation for midterms and final examinations, both instructor and student sought help from the practice testing. A student's total classroom work, including his attitude and effectiveness in use of the practice tests, did figure in the larger appraisal of him by the instructor, however. After issues raised by the practice tests were disposed of, further discussion took such direction as the situation to date suggested. This was to fill any gaps remaining in consideration of the subject, and to generalize and apply the material as a safeguard against the undue specificity which the objective study tests might otherwise foster. Then near the end of the second day assigned to a topic, a second practice test was given, with a little time following that for discussion. Finally, the day after the topic was finished, a 30-item check test was given in which 10 questions were repeated from one or the other of the practice tests, 10 paraphrased, and 10 new. Of the total 18 topics of the course, six scattered through the quarter were handled in this manner. The few minutes for the check test thus always came from a unit not given the special treatment.

The above procedure was used in two experimental sections taught by two experienced instructors who each had a control section, where as much time was allotted to discussion as was allotted to testing in the other section. In their control sections, these instructors were free to stress points which had come out in the punchboard groups or apply other helpful orientations obtained from the experimental procedures; except that the punchboards and practice tests were not used on the six units. The remaining 12 topics of the course were taught by informal discussion in all sections.

Selection of the two experimental and two control sections, from the total of all sections, was by chance circumstance. Their status at the beginning of the experiment was determined by an index taking account of each student's standing on the test of general ability given at entrance, his academic record to date, his grade in the preceding course in general psychology, and his score on a pre-test given at the beginning of the educational psychology course and anticipating the major topics of that course, to measure pre-knowledge. The experimental and control groups were found essentially equal initially, as well illustrated by the pre-test means in Table 8 to be presented shortly.

The first analysis was of the effects of the experimental procedures on the check tests given the day after each unit. Table 7 shows the percentages of questions correct in each group for all six check tests combined, or a total of 60 questions in the check tests which had not appeared in any form in the practice tests, 60 paraphrased for the practice tests, and 60 repeated from them. Analysis of variance indicated that in total the differences even on the "new items" between experimental and control groups could be considered significant. It appears that when such a diagnostic test-teach device is used as an integral part of instruction, results are substantial, and they seem to bring better understanding of the topic as a whole, so that even "new" questions in that topic are more often answered correctly.

It might be considered that the check tests were given too soon after a topic had been completed, and were too closely tied in with the practice tests. Table 8 shows the results of tests given later, having no such tie-in, and providing much broader coverage. In total, these covered all 18 topics in the course, were made up independently of the practice tests, and included an extensive case study test, unlike all the other material. Pre-test scores illustrate findings with a measure of initial status. Means on the pre-test are practically the same for control and punch-

TABLE 7

Percentages of questions correct on end tests, in two classes using punchboard tests as a regular part of instructional procedure, and in two control groups taught by the same instructors which took no practice tests.[a]

	No Practice Test	Punch-board	Punch-board Gain
60 Questions not in practice tests	54	64	10
60 Questions paraphrased from practice tests	58	75	17
60 Questions repeated from practice tests	60	83	23

[a] The two sections using no practice tests had a total of 57 students and the punchboard sections 62.

board groups, but on the midterms plus final the punchboard group is clearly superior, the difference surpassing the 1 per cent level of confidence.[8]

As in the appraisal of the review test in general psychology reported earlier, the design of the above experiment combined values of the punchboard and the practice tests. The combination was here also justified on the ground that the device so facilitated the frequent testing that values of the tests might be here included as part of the total value of the punchboard. However, evidence was again desired which would differentiate the effectiveness of the practice tests with and without the punch-

[8] As already mentioned, two instructors were involved in the above experiment, each teaching one control and one experimental section, so that any differences in their effectiveness might affect both groups. Comparisons of the means of the groups taught by the first instructor and the second showed no significant difference. The inference was that on the whole the two instructors did not substantially differ in the groups they had to work with, or in their efficiency. Analysis of variance also showed no significant difference between the instructors in the relations between their control and experimental groups; the practice tests with punchboards seem to have been used by them with about the same effectiveness.

board. The set-up now to be described was planned to take account of this issue.

b. Value of frequent brief tests with and without the punchboard. The plan was simple and straightforward. In the spring quarter there were 13 sections of educational psychology. Four of these used practice tests with the punchboard in connection with certain units of the course. They were taught by the two instructors who had just completed the project described above and thus

TABLE 8

Average scores made by 2 sections who had not taken any practice tests and 2 other sections who had taken practice tests on 6 out of 18 topics, on (a) a pre-test covering essential background and major points given at the beginning of the quarter and (b) two objective midterms and a final examination given during and at the end of the quarter.[a]

	No Practice Tests	Punch-board Tests	Difference
Mean score on pre-test	45.2	45.6	.4
Mean of midterms plus final	286.7	298.8	12.1

[a] There were 57 students for whom there were complete records in the first group, and 62 in the punchboard group. Sigma for the total midterm plus final score of the first group was 18.9 and of the second 16.6.

were accustomed to the use of the punchboard. Two sections took the same practice tests on these units, but instead of using the punchboards they marked their answers in the usual fashion on answer sheets. As they finished, they discussed the questions among themselves and with the instructor, thus arriving at knowledge of the right answers and clarifying doubtful points. The tests were then collected, and the answer slips graded and returned a day or so later. As before, this method probably leaned over backward in an effort to give full opportunity for advantages of the practice tests without the punchboard to be obtained; rather more time was given to test-taking plus discussion of the tests than with punchboard group, and return of the answer slips was a second reminder of the test and opportunity for discussion of them. Seven sections did not use these practice tests in any way, the time going instead for informal discussion. Initial status was again appraised on the basis of an aggregate index taking account of ability as tested at entrance to the University, scholarship to date, and grade on the preceding course in general psychology. Again the three groups were found initially so familiar that no allowances for initial differences were needed.

During the first four weeks of the quarter, five units or topics of the course were covered. The punchboard groups began consideration of two of these with a punchboard practice test which was used as a point of departure for discussion. They then took a second practice test on the second day, in the same fashion as the punchboard groups in the previous project. The test groups took the practice tests on these units in the usual paper-and-pencil fashion. The remaining sections covered these two topics entirely by informal discussion. And this last method was used by all 13 sections to cover the remaining three units. A 75-question multiple-choice midterm was then given all sections. Of these questions, 25 were repeated or paraphrased from the practice tests, 10 were new questions but on the same two units as dealt with in the practice tests, and 40 were questions on the three units not having practice tests. In similar fashion during the second four weeks of the course four units were considered, on two of which two practice tests were given to the punchboard and test groups. The second midterm was then given. It had 24 items repeated or paraphrased from the practice tests, 16 new questions on the same units, and the remaining 35 on the two topics which were new to all groups.

The bars in Fig. 1 show the scores made by the middle half of the students in the three groups, on these two midterms. The total scores from such varying types of questions are obviously the undifferentiated sum of various possible effects of the practice tests. But they seemed worth considering as evidence of outcomes in what might well become a common situation: practice tests used for some but not all the material in a course, and examinations which appraise students' work as a whole without differentiating portions so aided. The differences between the no-practice-test group and the punchboard groups are evident and clearly significant. Superiority of the punchboard sections over the sections taking the practice test

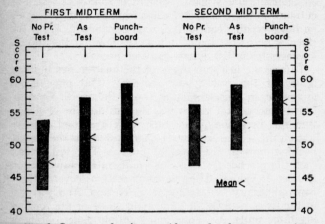

Fig. 1. Scores made of two midterms by three groups of students, those who had taken (a) no practice tests (b) practice tests simply as tests, and (c) practice tests using the punchboard.

There were 225 students in the seven sections not taking the practice tests, 70 in the two sections taking them simply as tests but with discussion after, and 132 in the four sections taking the practice tests with the punchboard. The bars show scores made by the middle half of the students in each group (from the 25 to the 75 percentiles). The practice tests covered only about half of all the topics included in the midterms.

without the punchboard is evident, especially on the second midterm. As always, individual differences in all groups are great.

Analyses of results are shown, in Table 9, for all the questions dealing with the units covered by the practice tests, and 10 items in each midterm on topics not so covered. The first three columns of figures show average per cents for each group passing each type of item on the midterm; the fourth column shows the gain of the punchboard group over the non-test control, and the last col-

TABLE 9

Percentages of students who had taken (a) no practice tests, (b) practice tests simply as tests, and (c) practice tests with the punchboard[a] who answered correctly various types of midterm questions.

Relation of Midterm to Practice Tests	Practice Tests			Punchboard Gains Over	
	Not Taken	As Test	Punchboard	No Test	As Test
First Midterm:	*Per Cent Correct*				
10 Questions not in the practice tests in any form, and on different topics	63	61	68	5	7
10 Questions not in practice tests in any form but on same large topics	52	60	62	10	2
20 Items paraphrased from practice tests	66	74	77	11	3
5 Items repeated from the practice tests	77	90	91	14	1
Second Midterm:	*Per Cent Correct*				
10 Questions not in practice tests in any form and on different topics	78	80	83	5	3
16 Questions not in practice tests in any form, but on same topics	65	72	78	13	6
14 Questions paraphrased from practice test	68	74	76	8	2
10 Questions repeated from practice tests	73	84	89	16	5

[a] There were 225 students in the 7 sections not taking the practice tests, 70 in the 2 sections taking them simply as tests but with discussion after, and 132 in the 4 sections taking the practice tests with the punchboard.

umn the gain of the punchboard sections over the "test control" sections.

The fourth column shows substantial gains of the punchboard group over the group which took no practice tests. On repeat and paraphrased items, the gains are greater than those for use of punchboard not integrated with instruction presented earlier in Table 6. In addition, the punchboard sections show superiority on new questions dealing with the same units, and even on questions on the units not covered by the practice tests. Apparently the discussion and teaching tied in with the tests, and aiming at generalization and application, had so operated. Moreover, the right-hand or fifth column shows some superiority of the punchboard over the test-control group; and this extends also, on both midterms, to questions on topics not covered by the practice tests. To what extent these last differences may be considered significant is not clear, but their appearance in all categories surely warrants added confidence in them. And again it must be remembered that punchboard testing was also more convenient, time-saving, and interesting to the students than testing in conventional fashion with discussion the next day.[9]

[9] The question might be asked: "Were the punchboard section instructors better"? Their "control" sections the previous quarter had been clearly below their own punchboard sections and at the average of other instructors; the quarter before that, before the experiment began, their sections had been no better than the others on midterms and finals. Might superiorities of both test groups over the control be due merely to greater habituation to tests? Present-day college students are used to tests; in the previous course in general psychology they are regularly used. Better scores on questions repeated or paraphrased from the practice tests would be expected, from students who had taken them, but should not be wholly discounted as due to undesirable rôte recall. After all, it is good instruction to bring up important points in class discussion, and sound testing that these points should also be covered in any later tests. And the gains on topics not covered by the practice tests remained to be explained. Apparently the punchboard tests, when integrated with instruction, brought more adequate coverage and generalizing of subject-matter than usual instruction—more even than the less convenient testing without them.

Doubtless there should have been a greater range of practice and appraising test material. But the experimentation included judgment tests, and a unique case study test. Earlier investigation under the writer's direction, with a basically similar device for self-instructional testing, had used true-false practice tests, appraised outcomes with multiple-choice and essay-type questions, and obtained similar positive results (Little, 1934). In total, the range in materials and methodology seemed considerable.

c. Student attitudes toward the punchboard. The above findings were the results of objective testing. Indications of students' attitudes toward the punchboard were sought. Their liking for it was well evidenced by their protest when, after its use part of a quarter, the experimental design called for its discontinuance. They found the device sufficiently helpful that they came to depend on its immediate appraisals, and guidance to right answers; thereafter, tests taken in the usual way, and leaving them uninformed in these respects, were frustrating. When opportunities were given to take a test over again, or to take other punchboard tests on the same topic (several were available on each) many students did thus extend their self-instruction. Punchboard tests were obviously a convenience both to students and instructors, for such use. Comments from students were invited. The following samples indicate something as to attitudes, and methods of using.

> Every time I punch a wrong answer, I read the question over again. The punchboard makes me think.
>
> When I have the right answer, but am not certain, the punchboard assures me; then I can settle on that answer and remember it, and consider the reasons why it is right.
>
> Direct questions help me; I don't retain as much from general discussion.
>
> My errors are pointed out immediately; I'm not left with the wrong ideas.
>
> New ideas and angles are brought out and underscored.
>
> It's like a game and a challenge; I'm motivated more.
>
> If you punch a wrong hole, you're the only one who knows it; it's not upsetting like a mistake in class discussion.
>
> With the series of questions and all the time finding out how much I know, I can concentrate much better than in ordinary study.
>
> After I've been through a punchboard test, I feel much more confident, know where I stand, have been checked up.
>
> I find it much easier to ask for help, since the punchboard brings issues to a head.

In short, use of an occasional punchboard test somewhat perfunctorily as a convenience in testing brought a little specific gain in learning. However, use which was tied in with instructional method brought decidedly more, *and* spread that gain so that general understandings were bettered and study methods made more effective. Further, under these circumstances, students liked the device and appreciated it as helpful.

4. Use of Punchboard Practice Tests with Special Groups of Superior Students

It might be assumed that a device facilitating immediate understanding of test material and self-instruction would be most effectively used by the ablest students. Since a class, like a fleet, tends to travel at the rate of the slower members, any scheme which releases the abler from that restraint should be valuable. Three methods of using the punchboard tests with groups of superior students were therefore tried.

a. The "Accelerate Seminar." An accelerate seminar was tried four different quarters. Selection of students for the seminar was based on a brief student data sheet filled out the first day of the course in educational psychology. This sheet covered age, academic record, veteran status, part-time employment, and interest in the seminar as briefly described to the group. Those students who were interested, whose academic records and scores on the entrance test of general ability were high, who were not over-burdened with part-time employment, and who seemed to have a reasonable participation in student social life and activities, were then interviewed; and the most promising were chosen for this special group. Average number in the seminars was 26, or a bit less than a tenth of the total 300 or so students taking the course each quarter. Average percentile of the seminar group on the test of ability at entrance was 77 and academic average slightly above B. A majority but not all were veterans.

The seminar met only two hours a week (usually in the evening) instead of the usual five one-hour sessions. All the regular readings and projects were covered and in addition about a third more reading, to compensate for less class time and assure against possible criticism that the seminars were too easy. Three or four punchboard tests on every topic, most with page references to the reading after each question to aid systematic check back on weak points, were made available to the students in a file, and they were shown how to load the punchboards with paper slip and key so that they could do everything themselves. They could thus use the tests for self-appraisal and guidance in small-group discussion, at certain class times and also at other hours in the afternoon when the file was open to them. Part of the class seminar hour was given to special projects or other undertakings and to informal discussion at a mature "seminar" level. And since class time was saved, each student was supposed to take an extra course, work part-time, or make other good use of less demand as to class attendance. Median course load was 18 hours, and median hours of part-time employment 10.

To determine outcome, students were given essay examinations upon the extra reading, were graded by the instructor on projects and participation in class discussion, and took the two objective midterms and final given also to the regular sections. The first rows of Table 10 summarize the results in terms of grades on these objective tests made by the regular sections, the accelerate seminar students, and cases in the regular sections paired with the seminar cases as to age, sex, point-hour-ratio through the previous quarter, and grade in the previous course in general psychology. With all these categories, pairing was a bit rough, but was reasonably satisfactory.

High (A and B) grades in seminar were over twice as numerous proportionally as in the regular sections, and failing (E) grades rare. Moreover, the seminar students were better than the paired controls, who had over twice as much class work. There were more intangible gains; many seminar students spoke of increased capacity for independent work, and closer relations with other students and the instructor because of the coöperative informality. The instructor found the seminars very stimulating. It was concluded that two seminars might be taught as easily as one regular section, making a net gain in number of students handled. Obviously many factors were involved. But it seemed clear that superior and well motivated students, taught in mature fashion, and with such aids to self-appraisal and review as the punchboard tests, could save class time and do more than the usual total of college work. Moreover, the demands of this course did not handicap elsewhere; a follow-up of these

TABLE 10

Grades made by superior students using special instructional methods including punchboard tests, as compared with grades of students using conventional methods of instruction.

	Percentage of Students Obtaining A and B Grades	E^a	Number of Students
27 regular sections	28	11	801
4 accelerate seminars	65	2	106
Cases paired with seminar cases	55	5	106
2 examination-credit groups	96	0	24
Cases paired with above cases	83	0	24
2 self-instructional laboratories	67	0	24

[a] A and B grades are high, but E is failing. Grades here given were based on two objectives midterm tests plus an objective final examination including a case study test.

students and their control groups about a year later showed the seminar group slightly more superior in academic record than before. And as a result of an extra course at the time of the seminar plus extra credit obtained at some other time, a considerable number of these students graduated a quarter or more sooner than would have been possible otherwise.

b. The examination credit group. Might superior and well-motivated students be put yet more on their own, with yet more guidance and help from the self-instructional tests? Two "examination credit" groups gave an affirmative answer to this question. University rules provide that a student may obtain "examination" credit for a course without taking it, if he obtains a grade of B or better on an examination covering the course. The question was as to whether superior students could, if given a little guidance in independent study plus the help of a series of punchboard tests covering the course, pass the educational psychology without any regular class work.

For this little investigation, records to date of students in the pre-requisite general elementary psychology were run over before the middle of the quarter, to find students doing exceptionally well in that course and otherwise superior. The best of those thus discovered were interviewed to verify as to their superiority, explain the plan, and see if they were interested. Only those strongly interested and clearly superior were finally included. Average percentile on the entrance test of general ability was 92, average grade to date was high B (a PHR of 3.35) and average age 20.5; preference was given to veterans. One quarter, nine students were chosen, and another 15.

As soon as each group was selected, near the middle of the quarter, the first of a series of four two-hour meetings was held. In these, procedure was further explained, assignments made in large blocks each covering about a third of the course, certain laboratory projects briefly demonstrated, and two objective midterm tests and a final given; there was time for a very little orienting discussion. In addition to the four meetings, the total series of punchboard tests was made available during about four hours each week with at least two hours' attendance required. An additional 20 hours each week was designated as office hours when an instructor or assistant was available for consultation and punchboard tests were also available. Work was thus largely independent study but with frequent punchboard test check, and opportunity for individual consultation. Often two or more students were in for the check tests at the same time, and worked together.

In the row labelled "examination credit group" of the above table, results are shown in terms of objective midterms and finals given regular sections also. The following row gives results for cases paired with those in this group as to ability and previous work, in the same fashion as for the accelerate seminars. Again results are excellent as compared with regular sections, but not quite as good as for the paired cases. Perhaps this indicates the students were approaching the limits as to desirable proportion of independent work.[10]

---

[10] Neither accelerate seminar nor proficiency group were without precedent. Worcester (1945), Munroe (1926), and Umstattd (1935) have reported successful trial of special sections meeting less time a week, for superior students, in several

c. The self-instructional laboratory. A third venture attempted even greater flexibility. At the beginning of two different quarters, small groups of very superior and mature students were given the opportunity to take the course in educational psychology in a "self-instructional laboratory." Each student was given a list of all the work in the course, including the usual informal laboratory exercises. Again a third more reading was asked of the special groups. Five afternoons a week, a special laboratory room was made available to these students, in which all the materials and readings for the course and a complete series of punchboard tests covering the course were provided. In charge was an assistant who was an experienced teacher and thoroughly familiar with the course and the practice tests. The students were told that there would be no regular class meetings. They could come into the laboratory whenever they wished, work with others or not, consult when they wished with the assistant. Each could progress at his own rate, test his understanding of each topic as he finished work on it, easily look up any item on which he had trouble (using the page references after each question), and then check himself again with a different punchboard test. When each student felt ready for a midterm or the final, he could ask for it. Each could thus finish the course at his own rate; all finished by the middle of the quarter. Results are shown in the last row of the table above. Over two-thirds of these superior and mature students made A or B grades. Some used the time saved in part-time employment, others in taking extra courses or yet other ways. Several reported gains in effectiveness in independent work.

In short, self-instructional tests made it possible for superior students to work largely or even almost entirely independently in various types of special groups. Much time was thus saved both instructors and students, and students' programs either enriched or completed sooner than otherwise.

---

different subjects. The University of Buffalo (Mills, 1936) pioneered in trial of intensive preparation for proficiency examinations. All the above studies reported favorable outcomes. The distinctive feature of the work at Ohio State University was the systematic use of the self-scoring instructional tests.

D. MAJOR CONCLUSIONS

The preceding pages have reported a variety of projects. What generalizations from them seem most important? Four major conclusions appear to stand out from the total investigation.

1. *It has demonstrated a simple way to telescope into one single simultaneous process the taking of a test, the scoring of it, the informing of students as to their errors, and their guidance to the finding of the right answers.* As stressed at the beginning of this paper, the usual test must be scored after the class meeting when it is taken. If the students are to know their scores and what their errors were, the errors must be marked on the test blank, and marked sheet and test questions returned to the class. If they are to correct their errors, they must find out what the right answers are. All these steps can be eliminated at one sweep, by self-scoring devices. Not only is time and trouble saved. Since usual test scores are not available until a later day, any use of those scores must wait till then. Self-scoring devices make possible immediate action. Especially in any situation where expeditiousness is highly important (as in a mass training program in a national emergency) such saving of time and trouble, and elimination of delays in use, could cumulatively be of decided importance. Irrespective of any self-instructional values, simple self-scoring devices should thus be worthwhile as a means for saving time and labor, and speeding up the total testing process.

2. *The investigation has shown that such a telescoped testing process, which informs each student immediately as he answers each question whether his answer is correct, and guides him to the right answer when he is wrong, does indeed transform test-taking into a form of systematically directed self-instruction.* Immediate outcomes of such testing with the punchboard appeared amply to demonstrate that this was so. Repetition of a self-instructional test brought marked reduction in number of errors made. These effects showed also on tests of different types than the instructional tests. The learning was primarily of the subject matter and not of the test key.

However, use of the self-scoring device in a college course as a somewhat incidental feature in occasional brief tests, brought only limited gains in scores on later objective course examinations; and these gains were confined largely to specific items covered in the practice tests. As with other teaching aids, self-instructional tests must be made a carefully planned part of the total instructional program, if their values are to be adequately realized. Their occasional incidental use must not be expected to show their real potentialities.

3. *The investigation has shown that when the self-instructional tests were used systematically in college courses as an integral part of the teaching method, gains were substantial, and sufficiently generalized to improve understanding of a topic as a whole—even help on related topics.* Thus used, the "punchboard" tests brought better work in regular classes, as shown by higher scores on mid-term tests and final examinations (even though used in only about a third of the course) than made by comparable sections of the same course not employing the punchboard. The device was found especially valuable with superior students. Sections of such students, using a series of self-instructional tests systematically covering a course, did superior work with saving of 60 per cent or more in number of class hours. There was thus marked reduction in amount of instruction needed, and the students saved sufficient time so that they could take extra work, many finishing their education sooner in consequence.

It appeared that substantial use of carefully planned comprehensive series of instructional tests could have advantages, over the same time in discussion, somewhat comparable to the advantages of an objective test over an essay type examination or an oral quiz. More questions could be asked, in a given time, of every student, covering a topic more systematically and adequately. The right answers in the tests could be very carefully phrased to be adequate. The wrong answers could bring up and then dispose of common misconceptions. Such helps as page references after each question could guide review. The self-scoring device brings all these values immediately and incisively. Both the experimental findings and the very favorable attitude of students suggest that all this was so.

In school or college, such materials should be of value as instructional aids in regular classes, and of special help for special groups. In the Services, particularly in a national emergency, the immediate scoring plus self-instruction should accelerate training programs. Special groups in officer training might cover more subjects or complete training faster. New training materials sent out to ships or to distant ports might be distinctly more effective, if accompanied by self-instructional tests. Programs such as fostered by the United States Armed Forces Institute might gain in both interest and effectiveness, if such tests were included.

4. This paper reports results with the punchboard. It was found simple and convenient even for student self-use, and could readily be made yet more compact and convenient. However, *the total project has shown that there are various promising means for automatic scoring and self-instruction.* A "chemocard" was tried. It was three by five inches and looked much like the face of the punchboard. Across the top was space for the student's name, the date, and like information. Then followed two columns of 15 rows of four circles, the rows being numbered from 1 to 30. It could thus be used with 30-question, four-choice tests. Each student was given a cheap fountain pen filled with a special red ink with which he wrote his name and other information at the top. He then marked through the first circle of the first row if he considered the first alternative for the first question to be right. If it was, the mark immediately turned gray (as a result of an invisible chemical printed in the "right" circle); if the mark did not turn, the student tried another circle in the first row, continuing until the right answer was found. Total errors was the total of unchanged red marks. The chemo-card obviously operates to test and teach in the same way as the punchboard, but the materials are simpler.[11]

[11] It is believed possible to print right circles with an invisible chemical such that any pen and ink can be used and the right answer will at once blur as in soft blotting paper. The idea of an invisible chemical to indicate correctness of response was developed by the writer's former student, the late Dr. Hans

A key machine developed on the basis of earlier work (Pressey, 1926) not only indicates errors and requires finding of rights before continuing, but also keeps a cumulative count of errors and can readily be used for repeated runs through the test to reach mastery. Yet another mechanism, again based on earlier work (Pressey, 1927), adds to the above features in that on successive runs through a test, only those questions are returned for further drill on which a mistake was made the previous time through. Such selective review according to each student's need should be yet more effective.[12]

In short, "human engineering" can aid educational and training programs by test-teach devices of various types. The major purpose of this project has been to evidence the value of the basic idea, as illustrated by the punchboard, and determine ways of using such a device so as substantially to improve instruction or training. The value of such devices, and the need for carefully planned methods for their use, if those values are to be realized, both seem clear. Research aiming still more to realize these values, and to appraise certain of the other devices mentioned above, is now under way.

REFERENCES

ANGELL, G. W., and TROYER, M. E., A new self-scoring device for improving instruction, *Sch. & Soc.*, 1948, **67**, 84-85.

LITTLE, J. K., Results of use of machines for testing and for drill, upon learning in educational psychology, *J. Exper. Educ.*, 1934, **3**, 45-49.

MILLS, H. C., Contributions of anticipatory examinations. *Studies in Articulation of High School and College*, Vol. 13, Series 2, Bulletin 1, Univ. of Buffalo, 1936.

MUNROE, G. W., Selected sections at double pace. *Purdue Univ. Stud. High. Educ.*, 1926, **27**, No. 4. Pp. 20.

Peterson and his brother, John, of Kansas State College at Manhattan (1930).

[12] This device would seem far superior to the Navy's well known "automatic rater." About the size of a comptometer, it requires that the right answer be found to each question before going on to the next, returns a card series to starting position by simply pulling a lever, and progressively selects for review the questions causing each student trouble, as mentioned above.

PETERSON, H. J., and PETERSON, J. C., A new device for teaching, testing, and research in learning, *Trans. Kansas Acad. Sci.*, 1930, **33**, 41-47.

PRESSEY, S. L., A simple device which gives tests and scores—and teaches, *Sch. and Soc.*, 1926, **23**, 373-376.

———, A machine for automatic teaching of drill material, *Sch. and Soc.*, 1927, **25**, 549-552.

———, A third and fourth contribution toward the coming 'industrial revolution' in education, *Sch. and Soc.*, 1932, **36**, 668-672.

UMSTATTD, J. G., Independent study plans, *J. High Educ.*, 1935, **6**, 143-148.

WORCESTER, D. A., Adapting to individual differences, *J. High. Educ.*, 1945, **16**, 152-154.

9

Knowledge of Results in Self-Teaching Spelling*

J. William Moore and Wendell I. Smith
Bucknell University

Three experiments utilizing auto-instructional materials were undertaken to obtain additional evidence on the use of self-teaching materials. The first two studies to be reported deal with the assumption that information on the correctness of each response must be provided to the student with a minimal delay (Lumsdaine, 1960).

In previous studies, immediate "knowledge of results" (KR) has been provided in a number of ways. In some cases, S is informed of a correct response by some mechanical or electrical device, such as a buzzer or a light. In other cases, particularly when the response required of S is based on direct recall rather than recognition, the desired answer is given to provide S with a standard against which to compare his response. In this latter type, both self-teaching textbooks and teaching machines have been used as the media for the presentation of self-instructional materials.

It is claimed that by utilizing self-teaching materials, a student may proceed at his own rate, and that he is in no way restricted by the rate at which his peers learn the same material. As a corollary it is claimed that most stu-

* This work was supported, in part, by the Susquehanna Valley Program, Bucknell University, through a grant from the Ford Foundation. This article is reprinted from *Psychological Reports*, 1961, 9, 717-726, and it is used here with the permission of the authors and the editor.

dents can learn a greater amount when using auto-instructional materials *ad libitum* than they can in "lock-step" instruction (Blyth, 1960). The question explored by the third study to be reported is, how is the rate of presentation of materials related to the acquisition and retention of the information presented?

EXPERIMENT I

Although there is some disagreement on the best method to use for providing S with knowledge of the accuracy of his response, most programmers accept the assumption that knowledge of the correct response with a minimum of delay is necessary for effective learning to take place (Skinner, 1958). A test of this assumption is made in this experiment.

Procedure: Two classes of sixth-grade students ($N =$ 62) participated in the study. The classes, which met in separate buildings, contained 28 and 34 Ss respectively. The range of I.Q.'s (Otis Form A) in the group was 67–123, with a mean of 100.42. To reduce the effects of pupil and teacher variability Ss were randomly assigned to experimental and control groups within each classroom. As a result of random assignment there were 15 girls and 18 boys in the experimental group, and 17 girls and 12 boys in the control group.

Fifteen units of programmed spelling were provided for each S during the last fifteen weeks of the 1959-60 school year.[1] To test the effects of providing for S the correct responses with a relatively short delay each member of the experimental group used, in addition to the programmed units, a small answer booklet from which he could obtain the correct response to a frame within a few seconds after writing his response. The control group used the same programmed units without the answer booklet.

The teachers[2] were instructed to provide each S with

[1] The self-teaching materials were developed by Douglas Porter, Harvard University.

[2] Mr. Guy Long and Mr. Bernard Zabarowski, instructors in the Danville Area schools, were the teachers who participated in the experiment.

a programmed unit on Monday morning during the regularly scheduled spelling period. The experimental group was given the answer booklets containing the correct responses and they were told to check the accuracy of their answer immediately after it had been written. Students were allowed 15 minutes to work on the unit; at the end of this time the units were collected. The same procedure was followed on Tuesday. No other instruction in spelling was given. On Wednesday of each week Ss were given an orally administered test on the 17 words included in the unit. All Ss were given the same word list used in the Wednesday test to study on Thursday. On Friday, they were tested again on this word list. This procedure was followed throughout the 15 week period.

All Ss were pre-tested and post-tested with the Metropolitan Spelling Achievement Test, Form R within a week prior to and following the experimental period.

Results: It was hypothesized that providing immediate knowledge of the correct response might increase the amount retained over a period of weeks. If this were true, it would be evidenced in a gain in spelling achievement between pre- and post-testing. Differences between the groups on the Wednesday test might be attributable to the use or non-use of the answer booklets. Differences in gains between the Wednesday and Friday test scores might be attributable to something akin to reminiscence, or it may be that mode of response interacted with the Thursday review of the word list.

Mean gains between pre- and post-testing were compared for the experimental and the control groups within each classroom and for two classrooms combined. The results are shown in Table 1.

It can be observed from Table 1 that the control groups were consistently higher in spelling achievement than the experimental groups; however, in no case was the difference significant.

In comparing the means for the two experimental and the two control groups and the combined experimental and control groups on Wednesday test scores, on only one unit was the difference significant at the .05 level. In this case, it was in favor of the control group. Neither the

TABLE 1, EXPERIMENT I

Comparison of gains on metropolitan spelling achievement test.

School	Mean Gain Control (N = 29)	Mean Gain Exp. (N = 33)	$t_{x_c - x_e}$
A	2.00	1.43	.37
B	5.57	3.35	1.18
Combined groups (A + B)	3.79	2.48	1.06

experimentals nor the controls were consistently higher in mean achievement score on each of the units.

In comparing the mean gains on each unit for the experimental and the control groups between Wednesday and Friday scores, significant differences were obtained in only one instance. In this case, the experimental group was significantly higher than the control group. A comparison of the mean gains between Wednesday and Friday test scores on the seventeen units combined again resulted in a *t* which failed to reach the .05 level of significance.

It could be concluded from this study that providing Ss with KR from an answer booklet (the independent variable) did not aid the learning of spelling. However, a number of factors which may have reduced the measurable effects of the independent variable are worthy of consideration. First, the mean number of words spelled correctly on the Wednesday tests was slightly more than 15 in both groups. When this is compared with the mean number of words (17) contained in each spelling unit, it is apparent that there were not enough words per unit and/or the level of difficulty of the words was not great enough to discriminate between the slow and rapid learners.

The failure to attain a significant difference when using the Metropolitan Spelling Achievement Test as a measure of retention may have been the result of the following: (1) all children were given the word list to study on

Thursday of each week, possibly reducing the measurable difference in the post-tests; and (2), although the Metropolitan Spelling Achievement Test may have some validity as a criterion measure in this experiment, a test composed of words taken directly from the units would have greater validity.

Since the programmed units were used in a text form, cheating may have been a problem. Specifically, it is probable that in a few cases Ss checked the correct response before writing the response to the item, thereby reducing the hypothesized effectiveness of the immediate KR.

EXPERIMENT II

Since the results of the first experiment were equivocal, a second study, in which more adequate controls were provided, was undertaken.

Procedure: A class of 28 sixth-grade students were chosen as Ss for the experiment. To approximate the population of Experiment I as nearly as possible, this study was initiated one year later in one of the same classrooms with one of the same teachers as in the first experiment. The Ss attending the school were from the same geographic area as were the students of the preceeding year.

The 28 sixth-grade students were randomly assigned to the experimental and control groups with equal numbers of boys and girls in each group. The chronological age ranged from 11 years 2 months to 14 years 3 months, with a mean age of 12 years 1 month. The I.Q.'s (Otis Form B) for the group ranged from 81–128 with a mean of 107.31. After random assignment of the groups the mean I.Q.'s of the two groups were compared by a t-test analysis. The means did not differ significantly at the .05 level.

A spelling test consisting of the 400 words from the original spelling list was administered to the Ss approximately three months before the experiment began. From this test the 210 words missed most frequently were selected for inclusion in a revised form of the programmed units. To increase the level of difficulty of the task further, the number of words included in each unit was doubled. In the units used in Experiment I the number of words per unit was 17; in the revised units, the number of words varied from 32 to 39 per unit. As a result, six new units were formed, four of which were used in the four week experiment.

A pre-test, composed of a random selection of fifty words from the revised programmed units was given to the Ss one day before the beginning of the experimental period.

The programmed units were presented to Ss in a Foringer Teaching Machine (write-in type) to eliminate copying of answers. For the experimental group, the correct answers appeared in the window of the machine when the lever was pulled. The control group used the same machines and programmed units but did not receive knowledge of the correct answer. This was accomplished by placing masking tape over the window of the machine where the correct answer normally appeared.

The actual classroom procedure was as follows: On Monday and Tuesday of the first week, the experimental group worked with the machines. On Wednesday and Thursday, the masking tape was placed on the machines and the control group completed the unit. This procedure was necessary since only fifteen machines were available. While one group worked on the programmed material, the other group worked quietly on other subject matter. A maximum of twenty minutes for completing the materials was allowed on each of the two days. This provided sufficient time for the slowest Ss; for the brighter Ss, it was more time than was required. Upon completion of the unit, if the specified time had not been used completely, the student was instructed to work on assignments in other subjects. For the second week the procedure was reversed, i.e., the control group completed the unit on Monday and Tuesday and the experimental group completed the unit on Wednesday and Thursday. The procedure of alternating the machines was continued throughout the four weeks of the experimental period. No other instructions were given to either group except those necessary for proper operation of the teaching machines.

On Friday of each week all Ss were given a spelling test consisting of the words contained in the unit assigned for the week. For each test, the teacher pronounced each word, used it in a sentence, and pronounced it again.

On the Monday following the four-week experimental period, a post-test was given to both groups. It was composed of fifty words selected randomly from the programmed units.

Results: Means for each weekly test, the post-test, and combined weekly tests were compared for the experimental and the control groups. The results are shown in Table 1.

TABLE 1, EXPERIMENT II

Comparison of mean scores on unit achievement measures in spelling.

Test	Number of Words	Exp. Group Mean No. Correct (N = 14)	Control Group Mean No. Correct (N = 14)	t
Test 1	32 words	28.0	29.78	1.19
Test 2	37 words	32.214	35.0	1.217
Test 3	33 words	27.286	30.357	1.51
Test 4	39 words	30.214	34.286	1.367
Post-test	50 words	41.286	43.786	0.727
Total	191 words	159.0	173.429	1.17

It can be observed from Table 1 that the control group was consistently higher in spelling achievement than was the experimental group, however, in no instance was the difference in scores significant.

DISCUSSION

Since the results from neither experiment demonstrated significant differences between experimental and control groups, it may be concluded that providing S with knowledge of the correct response does not facilitate his learning of spelling.

Given a literal interpretation, it is possible to conclude that the effectiveness of self-instructional materials in spelling (Porter, 1959) may be attributable to the format of the material rather than to the use of a technique for providing immediate KR. This is not to imply that some KR was not available (and a necessary condition for learning) for the control group. It must be remembered that although the control group did not receive immediate KR by seeing the correct answer after they had responded, the words were used in later items. They could, therefore, obtain KR, though the delay in reinforcement was longer.

It is of some interest to note that in both experiments the means on the criterion measures are consistently higher (though not significantly) for the groups which did not have immediate KR. It is possible that seeing the correct response to an item before moving to the next item in which a similar response is required, might be a case of over-prompting. That is, the hypothesized beneficial aspects of KR in the form used in this program, may in fact reduce learning efficiency when the appearance of the correct answer serves as a cue to the next item. Specifically, over-cueing may reduce the active participation of the student, thereby reducing learning efficiency.[3]

Although the data do not provide direct support for the use of immediate knowledge of the correct response, a number of desirable attributes of programmed material were observed in the experiment. First, both the experimental and control groups learned spelling to a high level of achievement without the assistance of the classroom teacher. In the second experiment where pre-test

[3] Some support for the disadvantage of over-cueing or prompting is given by Goldbeck (1960).

and post-test data were available, the mean number of students who got each word correct was computed for each test. The mean and S.D. for the pre-test was $\bar{X} = 15.33$, standard deviation $= 4.22$, and the mean and S.D. for the post-test was $\bar{X} = 23.06$, standard deviation $= 2.649$. Second, the same number of words (as indicated in the first experiment) were learned by the students as in a traditional method to the same criterion level, with a saving of at least fifty per cent of time for all students. The bright students had even greater savings. Third, the teacher was released almost entirely from the responsibilities of dealing with the formal teaching of spelling, thereby allowing more time for other instructional activities.

In summary, these experiments support some of the claims which have been made for programmed materials in a classroom, but they question the need for providing KR as operationally defined in this experiment. It is suggested that the advantage of KR may be nothing more than an additional cue for the response to the next item. If this is the case, and the conventional KR method is to be used, then the number of cues within the items must be reduced; otherwise the response may become "automatic" with little learning taking place (Goldbeck, 1960).

On the other hand, the intrinsic value of KR may be of real worth as most authorities in the field of automated instruction have suggested. If this is true, then more research must be conducted to differentiate between the reinforcement properties and the prompting properties of KR.

EXPERIMENT III

There is little evidence resulting from current research in automated instruction concerning the rate of presentation of material to the student as it effects acquisition and retention of the material presented.[4] How-

---

[4] Coulson and Silberman (1959) made some attempts to measure retention but did not relate it to the rate of presentation of materials.

ever, the results of studies (e.g. Kimble, 1949; Hull, 1943) investigating spaced vs. massed practice would seem to offer some evidence in favor of a controlled presentation of auto-instructional materials. A generalization of this type can be made only on the assumption that the use of programmed materials *ad libitum* and massed learning have in common some of the same elements which effect learning.

The third study was done to compare the effects of completing limited and unlimited amounts of auto-instructional materials, in a specified period of time, on the acquisition and retention of spelling by sixth-grade students.

Procedure: A class of 35 sixth-grade students was chosen to be Ss in the experiment. The Ss were randomly assigned to experimental and control groups. There were 10 males and 8 females in the control group and 10 males and 7 females in the experimental group. The I.Q.'s ranged from 78 to 131 with a mean of 110.52. The mean I.Q.'s of the two groups were compared by a t-test analysis and did not differ significantly.

To compare the effects of (a) completing programmed units as rapidly as possible and (b) limiting the number of programmed units which could be completed in a designated period of time, the following procedure was used: Six units of spelling were programmed into a self-teaching textbook form. The method for selecting the words and developing the units was described in Experiment II. The same materials were used by the experimental and the control groups. Both groups also were provided with answer booklets.

The control group completed one unit each week. They were allowed twenty minutes each Tuesday and Thursday for the completion of the unit. If S did not require the entire forty minutes to complete the unit, he devoted the remainder of his time to other subjects. On Friday Ss were given fifteen minutes to complete a self-administering spelling test. The test was made up of sentences using the words they had used in the unit during the week. Upon completion of the test, the date on which the test was taken was recorded on the top of their paper. This procedure was used over a six-week period.

To measure the retention of spelling in the control group, the test which was given at the end of each unit was readministered six weeks later. A post-test consisting of a random selection of words which had appeared in all six units was given nine weeks after the last unit was completed.

The Ss in the experimental group were permitted to complete the programmed units *ad libitum*. They were given fifty-five minutes a week to work on units or to take tests on the units. The major difference between the groups was that an S in the experimental group completed as many units as possible in the allotted time while the Ss in the control group were restricted to one unit per week. If an S in the experimental group completed a unit in one period, he was permitted to take the self-administering test at the end of the period if time was available; if not, he took it at the beginning of the next period. He could then proceed to the next unit. This procedure made it possible for some Ss to complete two or more units and tests during each week. When each unit test was completed by an S in the experimental group, he recorded the date at the top of the paper. To measure retention, the same test for each unit was readministered exactly six weeks after each of the first tests. The same post-test which was administered to the control group was given to the experimental group exactly nine weeks after the mean time it took the group to complete all six units.

Results: The mean achievement scores for the spelling test administered immediately after the units had been completed for the experimental and control groups were compared by the t-test analysis. The means of the groups and the results of the statistical comparisons are given in Table 1.

In no case did the difference between means approach the required level of significance.

A t-test analysis was used to compare the loss in achievement (as a measure of retention) between test I and test II of each unit and the difference between the scores made on the post-test by the experimental and control groups. Table 2 presents the data.

TABLE 1, EXPERIMENT III

Comparison of mean scores on achievement measure in spelling.

Unit I	Exp. Mean	Control Mean	t
I	28.94	28.47	.38
II	28.39	27.29	.85
III	34.26	34.06	.17
IV	31.06	30.75	.95
V	34.22	34.81	.39
VI	36.82	35.38	.83

TABLE 2, EXPERIMENT III

Comparison of losses in achievement on unit spelling tests.

Unit	Exp. $\overline{X}_1 - \overline{X}_2$	Control $\overline{X}_1 - \overline{X}_2$	t
I	1.24	2.00	0.25
II	1.14	2.77	0.32
III	1.88	1.33	0.15
IV	0.53	1.80	1.46
V	0.94	2.25	1.22
VI	1.19	1.81	0.18

DISCUSSION

The data from this study do not provide any evidence that massed practice with programmed materials affects retention adversely. The failure to obtain differences may be a function of the kind of programmed material used in this study, or to the relatively short lapse of time between criterion measures used. This study lends some support to those who recommend that the student proceed at his own rate when using programmed materials.

One advantage of presenting material to Ss *ad libitum* was the saving of time. The experimental group spent a mean working time of only fourteen school days on the six units, while the control group spent the entire eighteen days.[5] Further, the group receiving material *ad libitum* appeared to be more highly motivated than the control group. This supports Skinner's views on the motivational properties of automated instruction (Skinner, 1958).

REFERENCES

BLYTH, J. W., Teaching machines and human beings, *The Educational Record*, 1960, **41**, 116-126.

COULSON, J. E., and SILBERMAN, H. F., Results of an initial experiment in automated teaching, *Journal of Educational Psychology*, 1960, **51**, 135-143.

GOLDBECK, R. A. *The Effect of Response Mode and Learning Material Difficulty on Automated Instruction.* American Institute for Research, Technical Report No. 1, 1960.

HULL, C. L. *Principles of Behavior.* New York: Appleton, 1943.

KIMBLE, G. A., Performance and reminiscence in motor learning as a function of the degree of distribution of practice, *J. Exptl. Psychol.*, 1949, **39**, 500-510.

LUMSDAINE, A. A., The development of teaching machines and programmed self-instruction. *New Teaching Aids for the American Classroom.* Stanford: The Institute for Communication Research, 1960, 136-173.

PORTER, D., Some effects of year-long teaching machine instruction. Galanter, E. (Ed.). *Automatic Teaching: The State of the Art.* New York: Wiley, 1959 (pp. 85-89).

SKINNER, B. F., Teaching machines, *Science*, 1958, **128**, 969-977.

[5] Actually, the two groups spent approximately the same amount of time on the units, for the control group, after finishing a unit early, worked on other materials. However, under conventional teaching conditions the class is kept together, regulated by the "average student" in the class.

10

Teaching Machines: An Investigation of Constructed Versus Multiple-Choice Methods of Response*

EDWARD B. FRY

Loyola University, Los Angeles

Teaching machines are defined as automatic or partially automatic devices which present a question or other stimulus to a student, provide a means of response, and then inform him of the correctness of his response immediately after he has responded.

An exhaustive survey of the related literature revealed that Pressey issued the first published report of a teaching machine in 1926. His was a simple mechanical device making use of multiple-choice questions. Later he and his students developed studies using punchboards that gave immediate knowledge of results to multiple-choice questions. Pressey believed the use of teaching machines to be in harmony with such learning theory as that proposed by Thorndike.

In 1954 Skinner proposed that teaching machines were effective and in harmony with such major learning principles as "successive approximations" and an adequate schedule of reinforcement (frequent rewards after small units of work). Skinner and his followers expressed strong

* This article is reprinted from *Automated Teaching Bulletin*, 1959, **1**, 11-12, and is used here with the permission of the author and the editor.

preference for devices which required that the student respond by constructing his own answer, for example, by writing the answer from memory rather than by recognizing and selecting one of several proffered choices.

The purpose of this study was to determine, if possible, which of the two modes of response was the more efficient for teaching a list of Spanish words and phrases to 153 ninth grade beginning Spanish students. A pilot study showed that when students were required to construct responses, better scores resulted on a post test but that a longer training time was taken.

The major portion of the study was conducted under several controlled conditions in which the variables of time and number of repetitions could be studied. Under Condition I, both experimental groups (multiple-choice versus constructed response) worked to a mastery criterion of two correct responses while working time was recorded. Under Condition II, both groups were stopped before subject mastery was reached, thus allowing them equal total working time. Under Condition III, the stimulus items (English words) were presented to both groups by means of a large flashcard, thus allowing equal stimulus presentation time and equal responding time for each item besides controlling the number of responses made by each student. Learning was measured during two post-tests, both consisting of equal numbers of multiple-choice and constructed items. One post-test was given immediately after training, the other after a two-day interval.

Results: Responses to the multiple-choice items all approximated the maximum possible score and hence did not reflect any significant differences. Constructed responses, on the other hand, showed significant results favoring the constructed mode of training response under all three conditions for both post-tests. Under Condition I, where time was allowed to vary, constructed responses took significantly longer.

Conclusions: Given the conditions prevailing in this study, constructed training responses result in more learning than do multiple-choice responses if the criterion of learning is recall. The literature has indicated that the use of teaching machines offers great promise in the teaching of many phases of nearly every school subject. Teaching machines enable one to make interesting application of learning theory and the results of learning experiments, and would appear to merit considerable attention from educators. They are excellent research tools for curriculum construction and psychological experimentation.

Where it is required that the student be able to recall the learning material unaided, and given the conditions of this experiment, constructed training responses should be used, even if training time must be limited.

11

An Analysis of Response Mode and Feedback Factors in Automated Instruction*

ROBERT A. GOLDBECK AND LESLIE J. BRIGGS
American Institute for Research

INTRODUCTION

This paper discusses a variety of issues arising in the psychology of learning as applied in automated instruction. As in earlier conventional learning tasks employed in experimental psychology, discussion of continuous discourse programs of the kind pioneered by Skinner (1958) conveniently can center around factors relating to (a) stimulus conditions, (b) response characteristics, and (c) knowledge of results, or feedback. Temporal and sequence factors involved in variations in these three sets of conditions become a focal point for much of the discussion of learning problems and issues. However, added richness in variation of conditions and sequences of events appears to characterize continuous discourse learning, as compared, for example, to paired-associate rote learning. This added richness brings increased complexity to attempted functional analysis of the learning process. And due to the nature of continuous discourse material and current methods of programming the learning, more

---

* This article is reprinted from Technical Report No. 2 of the American Institute of Research, and it is reprinted here with the permission of the author and the Institute.

complex sequences of stimulus, response, and feedback
events characterize the learner's activity for a single item
or frame. Thus, the analysis of such learning does not
rest complete with mere recognition of a written single
stimulus term, an overt response, and a simple feedback
signal, in that order.

Past conceptualizations of paired-associate learning,
though extremely complex in the theoretical or inter-
pretative aspect of the learning, in functional analysis
tended to consist of rather simple recognition of an
S-R-Reinforcement sequence for each pair of terms.
Since the concept of stimulus supports, now prominent
in continuous discourse material, was not present in
conventional paired-associate material, and since the brief
stimulus term was constant throughout the trials, overt
responses and reinforcement of them figured as the prominent factors in learning theory. Also, as the exposure
of both stimulus and reinforcement terms was rigidly
paced, the subject was presumed to be forced to be engaged, for each item, in reacting in turn to the S, the R,
and the feedback term. This simple, rigid assumption, of
course, ignores the responding processes actually taking
place covertly in the subject, and gives an over-simplified
appearance of orderly knowledge concerning learning as a
function of the overt response and reinforcement. Thus,
learning came to be carefully plotted out in terms of
response frequency as learning trials progress. Some richness was introduced into theory by considering interpretations of such factors as similarity, overt intrusions, and
other sources of variation in learning speed for single
items, but in general, the notion arose that learning consists of making overt responses and receiving reinforcement.

It is the view of the writers that the above conception
of learning is by no means adequate in understanding of
or arranging for the learning of continuous discourse,
conceptual material. And, even though this paper deals
with responding and reinforcement variables, the writers
view the stimulus conditions and the implicit and covert
behavior of the learner as prime factors in their tentative
conceptualization of the role of the selected learning
components discussed herein.

This paper is in part a reporting of some of the rationale development growing out of the first major experiment under the present contract. In this respect, many of the comments expand upon the reasons for conducting that experiment; other comments grow out of interpretations of results obtained (Goldbeck, 1960). In addition, this paper presents some of the views of the writers on matters which they believe require additional research to achieve further clarification and understanding of the factors in programming for effective learning. In this context, much of the discussion is intended to refer to procedures for programming of continuus discourse material along the general lines of Skinner's methods. However, the content of the paper is more generally intended to call attention to basic issues in the psychology of learning in order to enlist interest by others in further research and discussion of issues.

Initial learning, or response acquisition is the primary emphasis in the paper, although some of the comments are relevant to retention, transfer, and use of the learning.

The experimental study cited above, and this paper both represent considerable focus upon two factors in learning the writers consider of major importance. First, our emphasis upon implicit and covert responding departs somewhat from the more behavioral language of papers which place relatively greater emphasis on the overt performance of the subject. Second, our viewpoint on item difficulty and the effects of right and wrong responses differs from the view that learning cannot be made too easy. Our view is based upon our concept of issues of cueing and prompting, learning versus performance, implicit versus overt responding, and upon empirical data.

Regarding terminology, it is well to note that we distinguish "response mode" from "response pattern." By response mode, we mean the rather formal aspect of responding, such as multiple-choice versus constructed response, or overt versus covert. By responding, or response pattern, we refer to the total implicit and overt aspects of reacting, the former being not directly observed. Although experimental investigation of some of the learning factors we discuss would yield data which would aid in inferring the nature of covert activity, it appears that methods and techniques for measuring effects of these processes more directly are to be sought.

It is hoped that this paper will help focus attention on some of the many still elusive conditions of effective learning, so that further experimentation and communication may result in better understanding of and programming for effective learning.

AUTOMATED INSTRUCTION AND EDUCATION

The development of automated teaching techniques and the wide interest they have stimulated among both learning theorists and educators have contributed substantially toward bridging a gap that has long existed between the problems of learning studied in the laboratory and the problems of teaching in the classroom. This previous lack of a beneficial interaction of effort can be ascribed mainly to a difference in goals; these differing goals in turn prescribe a difference in both subject matter and method.

The primary goals of the learning theorist have been concerned with developing knowledge about the relationships among the variables of learning. Subject matter and methods have been selected especially to best achieve these goals. The goals of the educator have been concerned with achieving the most effective learning of subject matter chosen on the basis of educational needs. The methods selected have been those which were believed to produce the best results, judging from classroom experience.

Now that some of the results from the laboratory have been channelized into methods for effectively teaching classroom subject matter, in the form of programmed instruction devices, there has been established a common ground of interest and effort among experimentalists and educators. But, educators are still concerned with some goals that have not been encompassed by programmed instruction techniques. These techniques are not intended to supplant the teacher and all existing instructional methods, but to serve as an effective aid to the educational process. It is to be hoped, however, that the problems of the educator will continue to motivate the development of programming techniques that will free the teacher to play a more productive role in the educational process. The contributions of the educator should be of considerable value in both the advancement of programming and the incorporation of programmed instruction into the educational system.

AVENUES FOR CONTINUED IMPROVEMENTS
IN PROGRAMMING

The development of improved programmed instruction techniques can proceed in several different ways. On the one hand, it is recognized that the student and teacher view the learning procedure as an integrated process. Since the scientists, too, must be aware that the various aspects or variables involved in the learning process have their impact on the learning outcome in a combined fashion, instructional methods may be studied in a holistic fashion. It is thus possible to conceive of and develop a complete programmed learning procedure and compare it with some other proposed procedure in an effort to arrive at conclusions concerning the "best" method of instruction. Such an effort depends heavily on the ingenuity of the developer. It is quite possible that the most effective instructional methods will be derived in this manner. Certainly, eventual adoption and use of instructional methods should depend on some such comparison of complete methods.

On the other hand, it should be apparent that the development of "complete methods" benefits from the theoretical analysis of the learning process into its components and the empirical evidence from studies which deal with these components at a relatively specific level. Auto-instructional methods and programs already prepared are largely based on such previous analyses and experiments. Modifications and improvements of existing techniques will benefit from further analysis and experiments conceived within the framework established by these recently developed techniques. Studies of interactions of single factors in various technique combinations are an important aspect of such research. The improvement may come from an emphasis on those features which are found to contribute heavily to the learning results or from data suggesting de-emphasis and perhaps elimination of those features which do not contribute to learning success and which may, in fact, degrade the learning process. Findings which lead to new concepts and, hence, to new versions of techniques are an even more important contribution that can result.

THE FOCI OF NEEDED STUDY

There are four major focal points of the learning process as it occurs with programmed instruction:

1. Learning material presented
2. Response required
3. Feedback supplied
4. More learning material presented

There are many variations possible in the operations specified for the student to perform at each of these points, and variations in the combinations of operations. Specifying a particular set of operations defines the characteristics of the auto-instructional program to be used. There are currently two contrasting points of view concerning what the characteristics of programming should be.

Skinner and his followers hold that precise control should be maintained over the student's pattern of responding so that desired responses can be shaped by a process of careful reinforcement in some successive approximation sequence of learning frames. It is done in a fashion which avoids rote learning and provides understanding by eliciting the desired stimulus-response connection under a variety of conditions.

Pressey, Crowder, and others hold that the student's pattern of responding should be stimulated to the limits of his capability. This concept of programmed instruction emphasizes the thinking or less controlled and more implicit responses that occur during learning. Feedback is provided for multiple-choice responses to reinforce and augment successful learning, to redirect the study process, if necessary, and to correct errors.

The many possible variations in the four focal points of programmed instruction and their combinations, each representing a particular instructional technique, involve responses and feedback which are covert and uncontrolled to some degree, whether they lean toward the shaping concept or the "thinking" concept.

A major task which the writers believe to be necessary is to untangle the specific variables that have been associated with particular instructional techniques and to relate these variables to learning outcomes. It is believed that such relationships depend rather heavily on the covert and implicit activities of the student and that the delineation and manipulation of variables should be undertaken with a recognition that active participation of the student is not restricted to reading what is presented to him and writing symbols or words in the spaces provided.

RESPONSE MAKING AND FEEDBACK

The remainder of the present discussion will be concerned primarily with points (2) and (3)—response making and feedback. But, as will be apparent throughout this paper, consideration of the effective use of these variables is closely associated with the form of the learning material, especially in terms of the cueing or prompting characteristics. One outstanding characteristic of most programmed material is its orientation to the student and his learning characteristics. Material has been written so that the student will be able to follow and understand each item of information as it is presented. This orientation has been maintained by using the criterion of student response as the guiding principle for preparation and revision of material. This emphasis on successful student response in preparing material, aside from the use of response making and feedback during learning, may be credited for a substantial portion of the success that programmed instruction has achieved to date.

A consideration of how response making and feedback should be used in programmed instruction to produce the desired learning outcome requires some delineation of the characteristics and descriptive dimensions of response and feedback. These characteristics can then be examined for the ways in which they may be employed to contribute to the learning outcome. It should be emphasized again, however, that the operationally defined conditions of responding and feedback may have implications for producing student behavior in addition to the activities explicitly required by the program. These may be mediators of the learning required or they may have such independent effects as keeping up effort, increasing concentration, maintaining alertness, etc. For work proposed in 1961, one goal is development of improved methods for study of implicit responses. Some of this behavior can be observed and measured if appropriate conditions are employed. For example, study of eye movements of subjects should help estimate time used in sequences of actions such as reading, re-reading, thinking, and response writing. Eye movement studies have been made to understand and improve reading, and to learn how subjects scan a work of art. Records of such movements could be useful to show scanning of stimulus materials, viewing feedback terms, glancing back at written answers, etc. With appropriate apparatus, this could be a valuable form of investigation under controlled or paced lessons, as well as for study of individual differences in a less structured program performance. Sub-vocal throat activity also might be useful to supplement other methods of observation and measurement.

Certain aspects of implicit behavior may not be amenable to direct observational techniques and must be inferred from behavior which can be measured. The student's own implicit responses may range far beyond the stimulus materials, reaching back in time to make new associations and forward in time, possibly in anticipation of the next frame, the test to follow, or in making inventive responses not measured in terms of the criteria or learning outcomes planned by the programmer. Arousing such desirable, implicit activity may be more significant in reaching the defined criterion than are overt perfunctory responses. Also, these implicit activities may be useful in invention, transfer, etc.

Methods for Producing Desired Responses: Control of behavior, it would appear, has been approached in the past through many different methods and techniques. The methods used in psychology have changed through the years, and they do, without doubt, vary in effectiveness. The methods used also have historically varied somewhat systematically with the nature of the material to be learned. The theory of learning developed has reflected the methods and materials used in the attempts to control behavior by experimental conditions. Some of the typical methods, and resulting emphases in theory, may be summarized as follows:

1. *The Confirmation Method.* This method, typically used in memory drum experiments, presented a stimulus (S) and required the subject to attempt to make a response (R), after which the correct response term was exposed. No hint or cue beyond the "bare" S was given. On the first trial, the subject had no logical basis for a response, the S and R terms being arbitrarily paired, and "meaningless" in themselves. The first trial thus serves as an "exposure" trial, or a special form of prompting trial to start the learning. On succeeding trials, many overt errors were made due to the length and difficulty of the task and the absence of "stimulus supports." Learning over a number of trials thus rested on frequency of exposure, and number of times correct responses were reinforced or "confirmed" and incorrect responses "corrected" by feedback. As some tasks required stimulus learning, response learning, and associative learning, the task was hard to master under the condition of *confirmation*. This procedure often has been called the "anticipation" procedure, as the subject attempts to give the correct response before the device presents the confirmation (or correction) term.

2. *The Prompting Method.* By changing the sequence of events in a paired-associate task from stimulus-response-confirmation to stimulus-prompt-response, Cook (1956; 1958, 1960) has found that the prompting method is superior to the confirmation method. After exposure of the stimulus term, the "response term" is exposed; then the subject views the response term and copies it. The superiority of the prompting method has been accepted by many only with difficulty, due to the knowledge of the traditional confirmation method, which interprets learn-

ing as making of responses without direct aid on each item as it is exposed, and having them reinforced. The prompting method appears to many a less "active" method of learning, and thus goes contrary to the belief that learning must be an effortful and unpleasant experience in which the subject is pitted against the experimenter, who has arranged difficult conditions for the subject to master. In a recent study, it further has been found that prompting in only three trials out of four is superior to either prompting or confirmation alone on every trial (Angell and Lumsdaine, 1960). Thus, prompting for each "item" separately over a number of trials is superior to the more gross prompt represented by Trial 1 in a confirmation condition, and the haphazard prompt represented by the presentation of the response term when the subject has failed to "anticipate." And, as Angell and Lumsdaine show, performing without the prompt on every fourth trial represents sufficient prompting, but not over-prompting. This indication that too much prompting can be given (the task can be made too easy) is important. It may be noted that, in continuous discourse material, prompting can be reduced by not having a prompt term on some "review" items, or by using an indirect cue (weaker prompt) in place of the exact response term as a prompt.

3. *The Cue and Context Method.* In Skinner-type programs, responses are often prompted, as in Cook's experiments, by presenting the response word before asking the subject to write it. Also, less direct forms of prompt words are used. These the present writers call "cues" (Briggs, 1960). Cues may be synonyms of the response term, indirect hints, or other semantic helps of various forms. In continuous discourse programs, in addition to prompt words and cue words, there also is the total context of prose of which the cues and prompts are parts. Thus, some words in the frame ask the question to be answered, some give background information, and some are the "stimulus supports" to help the subject construct the response. The total sequence of material is written to change the stimulus context of the responses in order to promote understanding or generalization.

The cue and context aspects of programming of course

are generally employed to achieve conceptual learning rather than rote memorization. Thus, the objective of the program differs from the usual paired-associate condition. The point is that "programmed" material exercises more "control" than a textbook because the cues and prompts are carefully arranged and overt responding is required. This probably serves to focus effort and attention upon each "frame" of the program, and prevents inattentive reading.

4. *The Shaping Method*. Skinner has employed the concept of shaping in discussion of both human and animal learning. In the case of an animal, a reinforcement is given for any overt response which is "in the right direction," or is only partially a step toward the required response. Reinforcement continues as the animal makes increasingly adequate responses. In contrast to Skinner's verbal programming methods, stimulus supports are not normally employed for animals. The first behavior of the animal in the experimental box is thus considered emitted behavior, in the sense that no signal is given to stimulate the animal to move about or to seek food, etc. Thus, the experimenter puts the animal in a special environment and waits for the animal to do something before the training (reinforcement) begins.

In verbal programs, there is not this same deliberate effort to reinforce only "partly right" responses. Direct signals to perform are given, and stimulus supports (cues and prompts) are employed to guide the behavior so that each response will be right, even if it represents learning of only a small part of a total lesson. Whether the term shaping should be employed in both situations appears somewhat doubtful.

5. *Reading and Selective Test and Review*. Normal study methods often consist of rather aimless reading, with only perfunctory effort by the student to select important points, to repeat them in review, or to organize the material in outlines or notes. Pressey developed his testing-teaching devices to improve study by calling attention to important points covered in the reading material and by presenting questions to be answered. The simple devices used with the questions provided confirmation-correction, and encouraged the student to correct errors

by repeated trials or by re-reading relevant portions of the study material. Thus, the total reading material formed the context and presented the background stimuli. The test stimuli required the student to recall and select for himself the information from the reading which is most relevant to the answering of the question. Questions were not usually interspersed into the reading material as in Skinner's programs, thus placing more dependence on the student's study efforts for effective use of the tests. These methods may be characterized as less controlled, as the reading units were large and the reading more or less separated from the question answering. In a sense, however, the method required more "construction" or "structuring" by the learner than do Skinner's programs, even though a multiple-choice test format was employed.

Response Frequency: If one of the values of response making is to elicit active learning, it is reasonable to ask how much response making is necessary. Making overt responses may be considered as simply providing a general set to participate actively in the learning situation. From this point of view, perhaps only an occasional response is sufficient to maintain interest. It is not suggested that an experiment be conducted to explore the range of response frequencies in order to determine some optimum rate of responding. It is likely that the subject matter would influence whatever rate would be most effective. Each sub-topic introduced might be the best occasion for a response with some material, while other units might be most appropriate for different types of material. It is worth noting parenthetically that a response for each sentence would have the effect discussed previously of causing preparation of material to focus on student reaction, rather than on the text writer's mode of thinking.

It is possible, of course, that too many responses can be required. Aside from the aversions that can result from too much of a good thing, increasing response frequency to a point at which little or no benefit is gained reduces learning efficiency due to the time required for response making. If feedback is provided after each response, the problem of increased time is intensified. If feedback is provided after a group of responses, there arise the possible problems associated with delayed reinforcement for early responses, and the effect of this delay upon correctness of later responses.

For students who already are inclined toward reading effectively and with "good concentration," the introduction of response making may constitute more of a disruption of the learning process than an inducement for active learning. A trade-off in effects may be involved between frequent response making in programs versus continuity in thought. Skinner has adopted the technique of showing "panels" which contain outlines, basic formulae or definitions, or other materials of a general nature. These "panels" are present to view during the regular sequence of program events and may mitigate the possible discontinuity caused by response making as well as afford aid to the student in making correct responses. They also lend "structure" and may thus enhance understanding and rate of progress through the program.

Response Relevance: Frequency of response making raises the consideration of response relevancy. The response may be an important term which is critical to the learning outcome or a term which has little or no bearing on what is to be learned. While it would seem apparent that choice of the response terms to be used is a most critical aspect of programming, the value of response making *per se* can be evaluated by requiring such perfunctory responses as articles, conjunctions, and other routine parts of sentences.

Responding with perfunctory or non-crucial words certainly could tend to increase the rate of progressing through a program, and may lend readiness to read effectively a key word to follow. In general, however, it is likely that the subject matter or desired learning outcome determines the importance of response relevancy. The more the response term is identified with or synonymous with the desired learning outcome, the more important should become the requirement of a relevant response. Even if the response term does not constitute that which is to be learned, highly relevant responses certainly aid the student in deciding what aspects of the learning material represent the core of what is to be learned. Even a signal to underline key words may have a similar effect.

Repetition: It is important to keep rate of responding clearly distinguished from response repetition. If the response term is closely identified with the desired learning outcome, such as in spelling technical terms, it is apparent that much advantage can be gained from requiring frequent repetition of the response. Requiring the same response to be made a number of times increases response strength with number of repetitions. A program sequence provides a convenient format for utilizing this principle of learning, and may avoid boredom as compared to repetitions in the identical context. Nevertheless, the nature of the criterion situation may determine whether repetition in the same or varied contexts will be most effective. Since this can be a very powerful variable, it is most important that, in establishing the importance of other variables, such as "size of step," there is no experimental confounding involving the response repetition variable. Also, it may be assumed that changing the context for the repeated response helps achieve transfer.

Size of Response Segment: Size of response is another variable which is intimately tied to the desired learning outcome. Spelling, for example, leads us to consider smaller response units than would English compositions. Nevertheless, in our approach to any subject matter, we have the option of choosing the size of our response unit and the possibility of some systematic change in size of response during the learning procedure. We will not consider here the issue of part-whole learning. The size of response, however, is relevant to the occurrence and implications of making errors and to the scope of elicited response pattern.

Much has been said of the value of "constructing" a response, but this value has not been calibrated experimentally in terms of true individual-imposed organization of materials, brief effortful fill-ins, and perfunctory copying responses.

Many real-life performance requirements call for large

units of response, as in making a speech, building a house, painting a picture, etc. Perhaps size of response should be increased as subjects gain knowledge and proficiency in an area of study and performance. One learns to spell words one at a time, perhaps a letter at a time. Speed in handwriting later is developed, until spelling of words often drops out as conscious effort. Whether different learning conditions are required for these different skill levels has not yet been fully established.

Location in the Frame: The response may be required at various positions in the frame—from the first word to the last word in the frame. This position is determined generally by the syntax or logic of the material. Position may have other special relevance.

A response near the end of a frame benefits from all cueing or prompting in the frame when read in the normal fashion. All material in the frame is read with the motivation of having to respond correctly. The "reinforcement" follows the response with little delay.

A response near the beginning of a frame may be made without use of the response aids which follow it. Or the following material may be read until the response is brought to threshold. That is, the response requirement may establish a specific set to acquire the information needed to make the response. The response can be made as soon as it becomes sufficiently cued for that student (a device for supply close-to-threshold response aid). This may result in a unique read-study sequence through the frame material for a student. If material following the response is read or re-read after the response is made, it would result in a delay in the reinforcement.

If more than one response is required in a frame, the relationships of response position and of response function become more involved. One interesting possibility is that multiple blanks in a frame may lead to overt responses in opening portions which become more powerful cues to 'the final response than these same words written into the frame. Thus, a successful constructed response may be a more direct prompt than supplying the word in the program. But, if the response asked for early in the frame cannot be made correctly, it may be better that the word were supplied in the program.

More generally, it is possible that an initial fast reading of the program preceding a second trial to fill in the blanks would employ the whole first (reading) trial as a cue for the correct responses on trial 2. If this were found successful, reduced cueing may be usable. Another possibility is that the subject should write the response if he believes he knows the answer, but "peek" at the feedback term if he is uncertain.

Remoteness of Prompts: A study now is being planned to determine whether moving prompts and cues to an early frame, but requiring a response in a later frame, is more effective than having the prompt present to view at the time the response is required.

Having responses depend on learning material that is not available to the student at the time the response is required should motivate him to read material carefully and thoroughly with more than the goal only to make a particular correct response. This advantage is in contrast to shaping a particular response.

Response and Feedback Relationships: Different combinations of response conditions and feedback conditions may shift the emphasis from whether it is the reading of stimulus (learning) material, the making of explicit responses, the making of implicit responses, or the receiving of feeding-back that is most critical or important in producing the desired learning. A basic point here is that, in evaluating the effects of a response variable or a feedback variable, it is necessary to identify what other program characteristics seems to have been associated with this variable by programmers, and to determine whether association is invariant. If the associated program characteristics are found to be tied necessarily with the variable under consideration, that variable must be related to both performance criteria and format criteria—with the latter involving variables which can, in turn, be related to performance criteria.

Form of Response: It is quite likely, however, that we will find that, in many cases, there is no basis for believing that a fixed combination of variables is universally optimum. Consider as an example the form of response required. The response may assume a wide variety of forms. It may be written, spoken, throught, constructed, selected, etc. There has been much controversy over whether a written constructed response is preferable to a response selected from a set of multiple-choice alternatives. These two forms of responding have been associated with specific characteristics of learning material presentation and with specific kinds of feedback that are possible. It is feasible, however, to consider the multiple-choice alternatives as a form of cueing or prompting. Many students may, in fact, develop their own set of response alternatives from which to select when none are formally provided as such. Conversely, when the multiple-choice alternatives are provided, the student may construct a response before proceeding to "select" one. Also, the selection could be indicated by writing out one of the alternatives instead of by making some more simple motor response. To break down the apparent fixed differences implied by these two forms of responding even further, we might introduce the familiar "none of the above" as an alternative.

It is contended that form of response can be studied as a variable under conditions which free it from many of the closely related issues of programming and which will allow a more useful evaluation of the criterion situations for which various response forms are useful. Whereas large steps and multiple-choice format have been associated historically in Pressey's procedures, while small steps and constructed response characterize Skinner's methods, there is no obvious reason why these particular combinations should be maintained.

Response Difficulty: The ease with which a student is able to make the correct response is a point deserving of special attention. Response difficulty is another variable which has engendered much controversy. One view is that a correct response cannot be made too easy for the subject. A second view is that the item should be difficult, but not so hard it will be failed. A third view sees a trade-off between the positive value of effort exerted on a difficult item and the negative effect of an error. A fourth view is that the experience of making errors and being required to correct them is an essential practical aspect of the learning process. For the sake of making program writing and program revision a simpler task, it would be fortunate to find either that making correct responses should be extremely difficult for the student, or that the student should have no difficulty at all in making a correct response. There is some evidence, however, that the optimum point of difficulty lies somewhere between these extremes (Goldbeck, 1960). A reasonable place to expect this point to lie is near the threshold for the response. But, how close to the threshold? Will it be found necessary to develop techniques which can bring different students to different precise levels for responding correctly? The answers to these questions depend very much on whether we find that the response made should always be the correct one, or that the occurrence of wrong responses is acceptable and perhaps under some conditions even beneficial.

The danger of heavy cueing to give a high likelihood of correct response is that response making may become an automatic activity with none of the advantages of active participation.

The danger of less cueing to give a lower likelihood of correct response is that frequent errors might also discourage active participation and that errors might lead to misconceptions. Corrective feedback is one important safeguard against the latter danger. An argument which favors a moderate degree of response difficulty is that the implicit response pattern induced by a challenging response requirement enhances the effectiveness of feedback information. Present methods of revising programs by tryout succeed in correcting items too difficult, but fail to eliminate items which are too easy. Perhaps a systematically programmed combination of response difficulties above and below threshold can provide the advantages put forward for each point of view.

Functions of Feedback: Much of the preceding discussion has touched in general on the role of feedback in programmed instruction. Specifically, feedback may serve several functions:

1. It may provide information concerning the adequacy of responses made.
2. It may serve as a reinforcement and reward for responses.
3. It may have a motivating effect on performance.
4. It may be used to direct the next step to be taken in the learning program.

In regard to the information characteristics of feedback, a correct response may be confirmed and an incorrect response simply may be disconfirmed, or it may be corrected. The confirmation of a correct response can be indicated by a simple signal such as a light or the word "correct" which can be used for all correct responses. The confirmation may contain somewhat more information if the correct answer is used as the feedback. This usage provides additional exposure to the correct response and, when used with written responses, can provide correction of minor errors such as spelling mistakes.

Crowder has adopted the practice of including an explanation of why the response is correct, thereby taking advantage of this part of the learning process to introduce additional learning material or to insure that the correct response is fully understood. There is another way in which some statement concerning the correct response could be used to provide feedback. The statement might not include the correct response or a direct confirmation of it, but could be written in such a way that the student would be encouraged to reconsider the stimulus or learning material and his response to determine that he has responded correctly. Such a statement may take the form of "If your answer means that 'such and such' is true, then you are correct." The advantage of this type of technique is to promote a more active and comprehensive pattern of student participation. The technique also should help eliminate the problem that arises when a variety of synonyms constitute a correct response or when a large-size response (e.g., a sentence) is required. There may be some parallel between this "indirect" form of feedback and the practice of intermittent reinforcement and use of subtle cues.

The simple disconfirmation of an incorrect answer is accomplished by some signal which can be used for all incorrect responses. The possible advantages of the disconfirmation technique are that the student is discouraged from using the feedback as a substitute for a serious attempt to make a correct response, and that it allows for the possibility of requiring additional attempts to respond correctly without the uncontrolled direct prompt given by the feedback.

The correction of an incorrect response can be accomplished in much the same manner as a confirmation: present the correct response, explain why the response is wrong, or present a statement that would not be congruent with the incorrect response. As discussed earlier, if the program is one which is prone to result in a substantial number of incorrect responses, the correction feature of feedback becomes a key point in the learning process.

The reinforcement or reward characteristics of feedback have been dealt with extensively in the laboratory situation and are basic to Skinner's development of the shaping concept for programmed classroom instruction. The establishment of desired stimulus-response connections by a process of systematic reinforcement of intermediate stimulus-response connections raises many of the considerations found to be relevant in the laboratory. The schedule of reinforcement, the specificity of reinforcement, and the extrinsic versus intrinsic properties of reinforcement are among the considerations for study in the programmed instruction format.

The motivating properties of feedback constitute one of the most powerful ingredients for success with programmed instruction. Finding that they are able to respond correctly consistently may be a strong motivating factor for many students, especially those who, in the past, have found learning to be a very frustrating experience. For students who have experienced much success in learning and who may have found that learning situations have not enabled them to utilize fully their capability for success, conditions which provide consistent reinforcement may tend to have a negative motivating effect. Regardless of such individual differences, there remains the question of for how long a period positive reinforcement will retain a motivating effect. Studies aimed at enhancing the motivating effects of feedback, especially on a longterm basis, are needed. Perhaps some reduction in feedback as learning progresses is consistent with another prevalent concept, namely that less guidance should be given as learning progresses.

The feedback term may have the function of directing or guiding the learning process in either an explicit or informal manner. The feedback can include the instruction to proceed to some later frame in the sequence if the correct response has been given, and it can indicate mastery of material in the intervening frames. If an incorrect response has been given, the feedback can include the instruction to return to some previous frame or to a special remedial branch of the program.

Even without the formal branching usage, the student can make use of the feedback to recognize the need to review previous frames or to adjust his rate and effort in proceeding through the program. Perhaps some of the complexities in branching format can be avoided by developing and providing the student with simple criteria for altering his progress through the program, in order that he may make most effective use of the programmed material.

POINTS OF EMPHASIS FROM PROJECT
EXPERIMENTATION

Results from the first experiment completed under this contract provide a basis for additional emphasis here upon some of the points which have been made earlier in this report. Rather than summarizing all points made earlier, the following items are selected for special comment.

The experiment, reported earlier by Goldbeck (1960), found that, for a program of discrete, factual items, the effects of *overt written* responses, *covert* responses, and *reading* responses vary in accordance with two criteria employed and in accordance with item difficulty. Three levels of difficulty were achieved by various degrees of cueing and prompting.

When retention test scores are plotted without regard for time taken on the learning trial, the overt response group performed poorer than the others for easy items, but much better than the others on items of medium difficulty. But, the overt group required more time for the learning trial, as may be expected when written responses are required.

When retention test scores are expressed as number of test items correct per minute of learning trial time, the reading group is superior for all difficulty levels of items. From the findings of this experiment, several comments may be made in the context of issues discussed in the present paper.

First, we observe that the writing of a correct constructed response in a program appears to demonstrate that some learning already has taken place, providing the response is not simply a copying response. The explanation for this apparent learning must lie in implicit activity. The writing of the response may or may not add strength to the retention of that which is learned, depending apparently on the extent of the cueing or prompting (Goldbeck, 1960).

The interaction found in the experiment between difficulty level and mode of response, in terms of a retention criterion, appears to be related to concepts such as effort, attention, speed of reading, and distribution of study time spent in reading, thinking, answer forming, answer recording, etc. The experiment failed to find overt responding with feedback a necessary condition for effective learning, at least for some materials and conditions. Similarly, we find that the making of an error during the learning trial does not always signify that the same (or any) error will be made in the subsequent retention test.

Apparently, the negative effect of some overt errors is overcome by the positive effect of some portion of the implicit activity preceding the recording of a wrong answer and by the effect of the feedback term. It is hypothesized that, when an item is moderately difficult, and effort is exerted to give the right response, a variety of implicit responding results, some in "right" lines of thinking and some in "wrong." If wrong predominates in strength or if strength oscillates, a wrong response may be recorded, but the resulting feedback is employed by the subject to confirm the correctness of the right implicit tendencies. In other cases of wrong overt responses on the learning trial, an error may be made on the retention test. A breakdown of right and wrong responses on the learning trial, for three difficulty levels, in relation to correctness on the retention test, has been presented previously (Goldbeck, 1960).

IMPLICATIONS FOR EDUCATIONAL PRACTICE

Methods of Programming: From a consideration of many of the programmed instruction variables especially bearing on response making and feedback, it is indicated that we are not ready to be content with any one "package" of instructional conditions, however much success and enthusiasm it may have enjoyed. We yet have to establish fully the relative importance of variables, the variable characteristics which contribute most successfully to desired learning outcomes, and some of the combined effects of these variables. It is also reasonable to expect that new variables will be identified and that more useful definitions of current variables will be developed. As our knowledge about the ingredients of successful programmed instruction techniques grows, we can apply this knowledge to the improvement of existing programs and to the development of new program techniques.

Combining of Molar and Molecular Approaches: While we may view the advancement of programmed instruction techniques as depending heavily on the investigation of the relationships between specific learning variables and desired learning outcomes, it is necessary to recognize that the course of experimentation will be affected by theoretical predilections and frames of reference. The learning experimentalists differ in their views on learning just as educators' beliefs about how children learn vary considerably. Some "good" teachers are said to be successful because they "challenge" students. Others are demanding in a way which provokes high student effort. Some lead the student through the problem. Others hold individual and group drill until mastery is achieved. Many use discussions to promote transfer.

One may see the "molecular" approach of emphasizing simple habit formation and the "molar" approach of emphasizing broader and more generally defined units of behavior in both the laboratory and classroom settings. Whereas the leaders in education have tended to exhibit concern with the more broadly defined aspects of learning, the contribution to education by programmed instruction techniques has been based largely on the laboratory work with relatively simple learning habits. Hopefully, both educators and experimentalists, each with points of view varying in molarity of approach, can reconcile their conceptual differences under the impetus to increase their understanding of the new instructional technique and to improve its effectiveness to deal with a broad range of subject matter.

Programming and Creativity: It is pertinent to point out that using programmed instruction techniques for effective learning of basic curriculum materials is not an assurance that these same techniques are appropriate for more highly "intellectual" or creative behavior. It is possible that different forms of programmed techniques must be developed for the different levels of education. It is also possible, however, that the learning techniques can be quite similar and that only differences in the programming of the subject matter will be needed. In either case, we must consider the effects of programmed instruction variables on how the student learns "how to learn." It should be noted parenthetically that such considerations also may be relevant to effective learning of basic curriculum material.

Although research is in progress to use programs to stimulate "creativity," we yet do not fully understand the processes and the variables which produce creative work. Some creative people have had no formal training, and have been reared in an intellectually "impoverished" home. Although some information must be employed in creative work, overtraining, it is suspected, may inhibit creativity if overtraining contributes to rigidity. Yet, professional people with much education often out-create untutored persons or those with "technician" training. The subject matter of education in the professions differs from that taught to the technician, with, we suspect, superior results. Thus, "education" is broadening in terms of transfer while "skill" training channelizes or controls behavior.

Some Unanswered Questions of Broad Significance: What are the implications of these considerations for "controlled" programs versus "stimulating" programs? Would "controlled" programs produce a generation of uniformity and inhibit activities which have not been programmed, but which may be needed to meet future problems? Would too much emphasis upon simple habit formation as a means of education inhibit new frontiers of thought? These questions will be asked by educators and the public.

Individual differences are known to exist, but evidence is conflicting as to whether differences are increased or decreased by training. If these differences are needed for the good of society, is there any possibility that there could be too much use of controlled programming? Or, to the contrary, would basic science be better mastered as a start toward new developments under more highly controlled education?

It is the writers' contention that obtaining answers to such general questions need not be restricted to the philosophical or theoretical level of inquiry. Experimental analysis of the variables involved in programmed instruction, of the sort discussed in this paper, will contribute to the increased effectiveness of programmed instruction techniques. This effectiveness, in turn, must be evaluated in terms of educational goals. Thus, a balance between empirical tests of programming methods and research to improve programming technique should pay off in the long run.

Lest the reader feel that some of the questions raised above contain too much of a "viewing with alarm" of the unknown longterm effects of controlled programming, we hasten to state that we advocate sufficient experience with the methods to help answer our own questions. Also, there will be certain checks and balances which accompany trial of programs. Normal procedures will not be abandoned overnight. Whether due to cultural lag or to wisdom, the first widespread use of programming in education will be as another tool to help get the educational job done. Thus, a "systems" approach, whereby programming is incorporated into total procedures where it proves most useful as a component of total methods, will result in a favorable balance of procedures. Eventually, educational objectives must be studied systematically in terms of methods effective in achieving them.

REFERENCES

ANGELL, D., and LUMSDAINE, A. A. *Prompted plus unprompted trials versus prompted trials alone in paired-associate learning.* Pittsburgh: American Institute for Research, 1960 (in press).

BRIGGS, L. J. A *survey of cueing methods in education and in automated programs.* Pittsburgh: American Institute for Research, 1960.

COOK, J. O., Supplementary report: Processes underlying learning a single paired-associate item, *J. exp. Psychol.*, 1958, **56,** 455.

COOK, J. O., and KENDLER, T. S., A theoretical model to explain some paired-associate learning data. In G. Finch & F. Cameron (Eds.), *Symposium on Air Force human engineering, personnel, and training research.* Washington, D.C.: National Academy of Sciences—National Research Council, 1956.

COOK, J. O., and SPITZER, M. E., Supplementary report: Prompting versus confirmation in paired-associate learning, *J. exp. Psychol.*, 1960, **59,** 275-276.

GOLDBECK, R. A., The effect of response mode and learning difficulty on automated instruction. Technical Report No. 1, September 1960. Contract No. Nonr-3077(00).

SKINNER, B. F., Teaching machines, *Science,* 1958, **128,** 969-977.

12

A Comparison of Several Types of "Immediate Reinforcement" *

J. William Moore and Wendell I. Smith
Bucknell University

An application of reinforcement theory has received particular attention from those working in the field of automated instruction (Coulson and Silberman, 1960; Lawson, 1960; Lumsdaine, 1960). Specifically, much of the demonstrated effectiveness of auto-instructional materials has been attributed to immediate knowledge of results (KR) as a reinforcer.

While the value of immediate reinforcement in increasing the rate of learning has been demonstrated, the assumption that immediate reinforcement (when the reinforcement consists of KR) as defined in the animal laboratory or in motor learning tasks is synonymous with immediate reinforcement through KR as used in a verbal learning task, may be questioned (Moore & Smith, 1961).

Most of those who have questioned the reinforcing properties of KR, have not questioned the general concept of reinforcement, but they propose that a distinction be made between *confirmation* and *reinforcement* of the response. Carr (1959) states that "confirming the cor-

* This preliminary report is based on a study supported by the Air Force Office of Scientific Research, Grant No. AF-AFOSR-61-54, and is used here with the permission of the authors.

rectness of a learner's responses to problems may be expected to be reinforcing only if the learner's motivation is intrinsic to the task being learned."

This problem is further complicated (whether KR is classified as confirming or reinforcing) by the limited amount of empirical evidence available concerning the effect various methods of providing KR have on human learning. For example, KR can be provided by (a) the immediate knowledge that the given response is correct (a flashing light for a correct response), (b) immediate knowledge of what the correct response should be (the correct answer to the stimulus item appearing immediately after the student responds to the item), (c) immediate reinforcement for correct responses using an extrinsic reward (a piece of candy or a coin presented for each correct response), and (d) KR provided by cues which appear in succeeding items (a normal condition in the linear program utilizing the concept of successive approximations for increasing the likelihood of making the correct response). In the last example, this method of providing KR could be in addition to, or in lieu of, the conventional method of providing KR in programmed instruction.

From the examples cited, it can be seen that methods for providing KR vary greatly in their reinforcing and in what may be called their "guidance" properties. For example, one would expect a tangible reward (money) to have greater drive reducing properties for some people than would the more intangible reward of KR.

Further, if KR, where the correct response appears immediately after the student makes his response, has only "guidance" properties, then this type of KR is unnecessary (assuming that the linear form of programming is being used). This is based on the assumption that sufficient cues should be built into the successive approximations of the items to assure a high probability of making the correct response.

The purpose of this investigation was to compare the effects of various types of KR in learning psychology from programmed material.

PROCEDURE[1]

Subjects: Two sections totaling 220 university students enrolled in introductory psychology for the second term of the 1960-1961 school year were randomly assigned to one of 10 groups. To reduce the effects of the teacher variable (there was a different instructor for each section) equal numbers of Ss within each section were assigned to each group. The Ss remained in their respective groups throughout the experimental period. To insure comparable motivation for all groups, Ss were told that a part of their semester grade would be based on their achievement on examinations based on programmed materials.

Experimental Period: The experimental period consisted of six weeks beginning with the second week of March 1961. The students completed programmed materials on a regularly scheduled basis, one hour on two days a week during the six-week period. In no case were the laboratories[2] scheduled on two successive days. All students were expected to complete 96 frames during each laboratory.

Experimental Groups: Since the amount of learning as measured by two tests of achievement could be related not only to the types of KR, but to the type of response required (i.e., whether multiple-choice or constructed), experimental groups were established to compare the effects of various types of KR on both multiple-choice and constructed-response items. Further, two more groups were established to compare the effects of teaching machines on learning.[3] In total, 10 experimental groups

---

[1] Our appreciation is expressed to Douglas Candland and Mary Jane Mordan for their extensive participation in the conduct of this experiment.

[2] Laboratories refer to those periods during which students worked on programmed material.

[3] Komonski and Eigen (1960) completed a study comparing programmed texts and teaching machines and did not obtain significant differences on the criterion measure.

were established. Experimental groups one (E_1mc), two (E_2mc), three (E_3mc), four (E_4mc) and five (E_5mc) used programmed materials with multiple-choice (mc) type answers. In group E_1mc-E_4mc the material was presented in a teaching machine, varying only the method of providing KR. In the fifth group the material was presented in a programmed text form with KR provided in the form of the correct response. Experimental groups one (E_1cr), two (E_2cr), three (E_3cr), four (E_4cr) and five (E_5cr) used programmed materials which required constructed-responses (cr). As with the multiple-choice groups, teaching machines were used with the first four constructed-response groups and a programmed text was used for the fifth group. The 10-celled chart shown here presents the experimental groups with the various conditions and types of KR.

EXPERIMENTAL DESIGN

Knowledge of Results	Multiple Choice	Constructed Response	
No knowledge of results	E_1	E_1	Only stimulus material
Immediate knowledge of what the correct response should be	E_2	E_2	The correct answer appearing after the response had been made
Immediate knowledge that the given response is correct	E_3	E_3	Stimulus materials plus a flashing light for correct responses
Immediate knowledge of results plus extrinsic reward	E_4	E_4	One penny for each correct response
Immediate knowledge of what the correct response should be	E_5	E_5	Programmed text

Facilities and Equipment: Two regular classrooms were scheduled for use by the 10 groups. Foringer write-in machines were used for presenting the materials to the constructed-response groups. The E_1cr group machines had black masking tape covering the space on the machine where the correct response normally appeared. This prevented S from knowing whether the response was correct or not. E_2cr's used the Foringer machine in the conventional fashion (the correct answer appeared immediately after S made his response and pulled a lever). The E_3cr group used a machine equipped exactly like the E_1cr group except that a small light was attached to the upper right-hand corner of the machine. This light was controlled by an O seated behind S and for each correct response which S made O flashed the light, signaling that the response was correct. If the light was not flashed immediately after S made his response, S knew that he was to move to the next frame. In no case did O communicate orally with S. The E_4cr machine-observers combination was exactly the same as the E_3cr; however, O kept a running tally of the correct responses. At the end of each laboratory period S was paid (by the laboratory proctor) one penny for each correct response. The E_5cr group did not use the Foringer machine but used a programmed textbook.

The multiple-choice groups used specially designed three-choice-response teaching machines. The programs were placed in booklet form to the left of the machine. On the face of the machine (between two rows of response buttons) an answer sheet containing three possible responses for each frame was placed. The Ss were told to select a correct response, circle it on the answer sheet, then press the corresponding response button on the machine. The E_1mc group used a machine which kept a record of the number of responses but did not provide KR. E_2mc used a machine equipped with three lights (keyed to the three choices on the answer sheet). The machine was so constructed that regardless of whether the correct response button was pressed, the light indicating the correct response would light. The machine also kept count of the number of responses which S made. E_3mc used a machine which differed from the

E_3cr machine in that it had only one light on the panel. When the correct response was made the light would light; when incorrect, it did not light. This machine was also equipped with counters which not only counted the total number of responses the Ss made, but also kept count of the total number of correct responses. The E_4mc group used a machine exactly like the E_3mc and was paid one penny for each correct response. This payment was made at the end of each laboratory period by the proctor. The E_5mc group used the same materials and followed the same procedures as the other multiple-choice groups. A record was made of the numbers of correct responses and total responses for each S at the end of each period.

Each laboratory had one proctor assigned for its general supervision (the distribution of materials and directing of Os). An average of one O for each three Ss was provided in each of the laboratories. The purpose of these Os was to make certain that the Ss completed the program as stated in the experimental design. The presence of several Os helped to reduce the "observer variable" introduced in the E_3cr and E_4cr groups.[4] In no instance

Materials: Eleven hundred fifty-two frames of the Holland-Skinner psychology program were used.[5] This program was selected because of the careful manner in which it was developed. The constructed-response portion consisted of placing 96 frames on each of 12 rolls of materials for use in the Foringer machine. One roll was used during each laboratory session. Since the conventional Holland-Skinner program is in the constructed-response form, a modification of the program had to be made to adapt it to the multiple-choice machines. This modification consisted of constructing three answers for each item, only one of which was correct. Otherwise, the programs were exactly alike.

No other formal instruction in learning theory was provided for the Ss during the experimental period.

[4] In these groups one O was necessary for each S.
did Os provide information about the program to the Ss.
[5] Permission to use this material was granted by James Holland to whom we express our appreciation for this courtesy.

Evaluation: All Ss were given an examination at the end of the sixth unit of material. This examination was administered in one of their regularly scheduled class periods. The examination was based solely on the information included in the six units and the test items were closely related to the items contained in the program.

At the end of the experimental period, a final examination was administered which included all of the concepts presented during the experimental period. It was made up of one-half multiple-choice items and one-half constructed-response items. This type of examination, in addition to being a measure of achievement could provide some information concerning the interaction between the type of response element employed in the program and the type of test item used in evaluating the student.

An attitude measure, in the form of a questionnaire, was completed by each S at the end of the experimental period. It was expected that this might indicate some relationship between the achievement, as measured by the criteria measures, and the interest in this method of instruction.

Results: Since this is a preliminary report, only data derived from the two criteria measures are available at this time. An analysis of variance was applied to the data to compare differences of means resulting from the types of KR provided, the method of responding, and the interactions of these variables. Tables 1 and 2 summarize the results of this analysis. Since none of the *F*'s reached the necessary level of significance it must be concluded that differences among groups are attributable to chance.

DISCUSSION

The failure to attain significant differences may be attributable to several factors. First, the evaluating instruments used as the criterion measures may not have been sufficiently sensitive to the effects of the various experimental conditions. Second, differences betwen and/or among groups may have been reduced by inadequate control of certain variables within the experimental design (e.g., the ratio of Os to Ss varied from one per S to one for three Ss). Third, the procedure followed by

TABLE 1

Analysis of variance of achievement test scores (test I).

Source of Variation	df	ms	F
Mode of response	1	33.49	1.16
Knowledge of results	4	59.99	2.09
Interaction	4	11.73	0.41
Within	177	28.75	

TABLE 2

Analysis of variance of achievement test scores (test II).

Source of Variation	df	ms	F
Mode of responses	1	29.60	0.17
Knowledge of results	4	372.11	2.12
Interaction	4	29.45	0.17
Within	180	175.48	

some Ss in working with the material may have reduced differences. For example, it was possible for those Ss who used multiple-choice teaching machines and programmed texts to refer to a previously completed frame (one of the functions of the Os was to see that this was not done), while referral to a previously completed item was not possible for Ss who used constructed-response machines (Goldbeck, 1960).

If the criteria measures were valid, and if the failure to reach a satisfactory level of significance was not the result of uncontrolled variables, then other explanations are possible. For example, the comparisons made between groups using the constructed-response machines with and without KR, are based on well-controlled experimental conditions. Two, or the combination of two, hypotheses may account for the failure of these comparisons to differ significantly. First, the "no KR" groups may have received KR in the succeeding frames (Moore and Smith, 1961). If this is the case, it could be questioned whether this type of KR was "intrinsically reinforcing." (For KR of this type to be intrinsically reinforcing, it would seem logical to assume that enough information would have to be obtained from the frame to provide absolute assurance that the preceding item was correct), or whether the KR was sufficiently subtle that it provided some guidance in answering the item but still was not intrinsically rewarding. Second, the group which was not provided with immediate KR may have been forced to respond more actively to the individual stimulus elements than the group which had immediate KR (Goldbeck, 1960). If this were the case, it could be assumed that this effect was sufficient to counterbalance the positive effects of the intrinsically motivating properties (if, in fact, this is a result of KR) of immediate KR. A further finding resulting from that part of the study in which better controls were possible, was that the groups using the programmed text and those using teaching machines did not differ significantly. In fact, the mean achievement scores on the criteria measures were consistently in favor of the programmed text. This finding has been reported by Komonski and Eigen (1960), also.

An interesting observation was made concerning the rank of the mean number of errors on each of the two tests for both the constructed-response and multiple-choice groups. It was noted that a smaller mean number of errors was made (rank) by the groups using the programmed texts and the groups which were receiving an extrinsic reward than was made by the other groups. If significance can be attached (because of relevant positions of mean errors on the criterion measures) to this observation, it suggests that (1) the teaching machines are not as an effective a media (in terms of learning) for presenting programmed materials as is a programmed text, and (2) an extrinsic reward (though in this case it might be better classified an incentive rather than a reinforcer), when added to KR, is more effective in reducing error rate on a criterion measure than KR by itself.

At the time of the writing of this preliminary report, a complete analysis of the data has not been made. However, an analysis of error rate on programmed material is being done, as well as a tabulation of the results from a questionnaire which was designed to provide an evaluation of interest and attitude toward the experimental methods used in this investigation. Comparisons will be made of the types of KR and the types of responses on the error rate of the programmed material. Comparisons also will be made relating error rate on programmed material and scores achieved on the criteria measures. The questionnaires will provide some information concerning the relationships between interest in the programmed material and the level of achievement defined in terms of error rate and of scores on the criterion measure.

REFERENCES

CARR, W. J. *Self Instructional Devices: A Review of Current Concepts*. Aero-Space Medical Laboratory, Wright Air Development Center, W.A.D.C. Technical Report 59-503, 1959.

COULSON, J. E., and SILBERMAN, H. F., Results of an initial experiment in automated teaching, *Journal of Educational Psychology*, 1960, **51**, 135-143.

GOLDBECK, R. A. *The Effect of Response Mode and Learning Material Difficulty on Automated Instruction*. American Institute for Research, Technical Report No. 1, 1960.

KOMOSKI, P. K., and EIGEN, L. D. *Research Summary Number One*. New York: Automated Teaching Project, Collegiate School, 1960.

LAWSON, REED. *Learning and Behavior*. New York: MacMillan, 1960.

LUMSDAINE, A. A., The development of teaching machines and programmed self-instruction, *New Teaching Aids for the American Classroom*. Stanford University: The Institute for Communication Research, 1960, 136-173.

MOORE, J. W., and SMITH, W. I., Knowledge of results in self-teaching spelling, *Psychol. Rep.*, 1961, 9, 717-726.

SKINNER, B. F., Teaching Machines. *Science*, 1958, **128**, 969-977.

13

Size of Step and Cueing*

WENDELL I. SMITH AND J. WILLIAM MOORE
Bucknell University

One of the common problems of a programmer who is using the linear form of programming is to determine the size-of-step between frames. The concern about the concepts of size-of-step and cueing is based on the desire to increase the probability that a student responding to any given item will make the correct response. The size-of-step may vary in at least two ways. It may vary in the relationship of a succeeding item to a previous item (the degree of change in the reduction of cues in the items), and, two, it may vary in the number of cues within an item that is not dependent on a previous item.

The concept of size-of-step, by definition incorporates the principle of cueing and it may, in addition, influence the rate and amount of learning through the frequency with which repetition of the correct response is required. On the other hand, the concept of cueing places less emphasis on learning through the repetition of the correct response in a series of frames, and places more attention on the eliciting of the correct response within a given item. It is on this basis that the concepts, size-of-step and cueing are differentiated in this paper.

The importance of this problem is evident when atten-

* This is a preliminary report of a study supported by Grant No. 736087, United States Office of Education, Department of Health, Education and Welfare, and is used here with the permission of the authors. (A complete report on this research will be found in *Psychol. Rep.*, 1962, **10**, 287–294.)

tion is given to the conventional methods of programming in the linear form. Usually the size-of-step (i.e., the number of frames included in the program) is determined by the slowest (lowest ability) test student used in the development of the program. The assumption usually made is that if the size-of-step is decreased to the point where the weakest student can complete the material with a minimal error rate, the optimum program for all students for whom the program was written will have been developed.

Some evidence is available (Goldbeck, 1960) which indicates that a low error rate on a program does not necessarily mean optimum achievement on a criterion measure. This suggests that providing larger steps (either by a smaller number of repetitions in responses for a given concept or by reducing the cues within a frame) does not necessarily reduce the efficiency in learning, although it may increase error rate. Therefore, it is desirable that more attention be given to the performance on the criterion measures as a means of evaluating programmed material than to the error rates for a program. This is not to imply that a relationship does not exist between the error rate a student makes on a program and the score he achieves on a criterion measure, but it does suggest that excessively small steps and/or strong cueing (to assure minimal error rates) may not produce the highest scores on a criterion measure.

The purpose of this study, therefore, was to compare the effects of three different sizes-of-step, amount of cueing, and the use of illustrations on the spelling achievement of fifth-grade children.

PROCEDURE

Subjects: Three sections of fifth-grade Ss were selected for participation in the program.[1] In order to have a popu-

[1] Fifth-grade students were used as subjects because the experimental period was scheduled for the last four weeks of the academic year. Since the spelling materials were based on sixth grade spelling lists it was felt that these subjects would be more typically sixth graders (because it was the end of the year) therefore the material should be most appropriate for them.

lation representative of the school district[2] in which the experiment was conducted, one grade each was selected from three of the four elementary schools. The 96 Ss were then randomly assigned to one of six experimental conditions. To reduce the effects of the teacher variable, the students were assigned to one of six groups within each room, thereby creating six experimental conditions within each room. The mean I.Q. of the group was 105.58 and the mean age at the beginning of the experimental period was 11 years 1 month. As a further control, the students were matched on the basis of sex before assignment.

Experimental Treatment: A list of 166 words was compiled by selecting words most frequently included in 13 widely used sixth-grade spellers. To compare the effects of size-of-step and cueing on learning, six different programmed forms of each unit were written.[3] The forms were: a small-step program (4–9 frames per word) in two forms, one with pictorial cues, and one without pictorial cues; a medium-step program (3–7 frames per word), one form with pictorial cues, the other form without pictorial cues; and a large-step program (3–6 frames per word) with the comparable forms as indicated for the first two programs. For pictorial cues, an illustration which was appropriate for each word was sketched on the program beside the word on its first occurrence. All materials were provided in a self-teaching textbook with a separate booklet containing the correct answers. The students were instructed to complete each item, then immediately confirm the correctness of their response from the answer booklet. Other than general instructions for using the materials, no assistance in the teaching of spelling was provided. All Ss were instructed to complete each frame and proceed to the next one without reviewing previous ones.

The total experimental period lasted for four weeks, during which Ss completed two units each week. The Ss

[2] This study was conducted in the Danville area schools, Danville, Pennsylvania. The cooperation of Mr. Robert Hauck, elementary supervisor, and his staff made the study possible.
[3] The programming was done by Mary Haupt Smith.

were given a maximum of 35 minutes for the completion of each unit.[4] Tuesdays and Thursdays were used by all three teachers for completing the units. On Friday an orally administered spelling test consisting of a list of all words included in the two units was given by the teachers to the groups. This procedure was used on all four weeks of the experimental periods.

In addition to the weekly tests, the Ss were pre-tested and post-tested respectively one day before and one day following the experimental period. This spelling test consisted of a random selection of 50 words out of the total spelling list.

RESULTS

To obtain evidence that the various experimental methods were effective in teaching spelling, the mean gain between the pre-test and post-test for all Ss was computed. The mean gain was 11.23 words. Since these tests were made up of a representative sample the spelling list of 166 words, an estimate of the total mean gain in spelling achievement can be obtained by multiplying the mean (11.23) of the sample by 3.33. The estimated mean gain in achievement over the four weeks of the experimental period was 40.96 words.

To evaluate the effects of the several experimental conditions on the Ss' spelling achievement, the means on each of the weekly tests were compared by the use of the F-test.

In none of the four comparisons were the differences between means sufficiently great to reach a satisfactory level of significance.

Discussion: Although only preliminary analysis of the data has been completed at this time, neither the size-of-step nor the pictorial cues seemed to affect significantly the scores on the criterion measure. This would suggest that the range in size-of-step and cueing from the small-

---

[4] The 35-minute periods proved to be a sufficient amount of time for even the children who were the slowest workers in the groups. If a student completed the unit before the maximum time, he was instructed to work on other subjects.

step-pictorially-cued program to the large-step-non-pictorially-cued program all met the conditions necessary for learning. Since the large-step program proved to be as effective in teaching spelling as the small-step program (and it could be considered more efficient since logically it would require less time to complete) it may be concluded that programs consisting of steps which are very small are not necessarily an efficient method of instruction. Further, if very small steps and over-cueing are interpreted by S as unnecessary repetition, then the additional hazard of loss of interest in the material may be an undesirable by-product. Since this is a preliminary report, error rate on the individual programs has not been computed, therefore, comparison of error rate and achievement on the criterion measure have not been made. If it is found that a greater number of errors was made on the largest step, unillustrated program than on the smallest step, illustrated program, there will be support for Goldbeck's finding that a low error rate on the instructional materials does not always yield highest achievement on the criterion measure.

It should be noted that all six forms of the program provided an effective method of teaching spelling without the assistance of a classroom teacher.

It is concluded from these preliminary data that the necessity for small steps and strong cueing to assure the eliciting of the correct response to the frame of a program may have been overemphasized; that larger step programs (an optimal level must be identified) may have greater motivational value, and they may teach as much as effectively in less time.

REFERENCE

GOLDBECK, R. A., The effect of response mode and learning material difficulty on automated instruction, American Institute for Research, Technical Report No. 1, 1960.

14

Automated Teaching and Individual Differences*

JOHN E. COULSON AND HARRY F. SILBERMAN
System Development Corporation

In 1958 an automated teaching project was formed by members of the Research Directorate at the System Development Corporation. The functions of this project were to investigate the current status of automated teaching, to conduct research on variables of automated instruction, and to determine what contribution SDC, as a non-profit corporation, might make in the developmental and applied aspects of this field.

Project members began with a review of the "state of the art" as it then existed. This review indicated that, despite an apparent diversity in design, most teaching machines had one characteristic in common: a relative inflexibility of operation. With a given set of instructional materials ("items") in the machine, each student working with the machine would receive the same sequence of items, regardless of his individual capabilities or limitations.

The basic assumption underlying the design of a fixed-sequence teaching machine is that a single sequence of items can be optimally effective for a number of students. This assumption seemed highly doubtful when

* This article originally appeared in *Audio Visual Communication Review*, 1961, **9**, 5-15, and is reprinted here with the permission of the authors and the publisher.

viewed in the context of the typical classroom, with 20 or more students differing not only in training experience but in inherent ability as well. It appeared that an ideal sequence of items for one student would be less than maximally effective for some other student.

Using certain behavior characteristics of the human tutor as an initial guide, project members considered possible teaching-machine designs which might use different instructional procedures for different students, depending on the students' performance during training. This adaptable feature was termed "machine responsiveness." It was clearly recognized that well-written, well-tested instructional items were essential for any successful automated instruction. Without such materials any teaching machine would be completely useless. Given a good set of items, however, it was believed that the interaction between student response-behavior and machine selection of materials might be an important factor in the effectiveness of automated instruction.

In April 1959, the Automated Teaching Project conducted an experiment with manually operated teaching machines to explore the effectiveness of machine responsiveness, as compared with a fixed sequence mode (Coulson and Silberman, 1960). Responsiveness was introduced by a simplified form of "branching" in which a student who correctly answered an item on a given topic was not shown other items on the same topic.[1] In this way each member of the "branching" group received a (different) subset of the items seen by the fixed sequence group. Other variables investigated in the same experiment were student response-mode (multiple-choice versus constructed-response) and item step-size (many small steps versus fewer large steps). Materials in elementary psychology were presented to 80 junior-college students. Results of the study were as follows:

1. Training with the manually controlled machines yielded significant student learning in each of the experimental groups.

---

[1] This particular method of branching was unquestionably crude, and the criterion for branching somewhat unrealistic. It was found, however, that more complex forms of branching were not feasible with the manually operated machines.

2. "Branching" students required significantly less training time than "fixed sequence" students, and did not differ on a post-training criterion test.

3. Students receiving many items with small steps learned more than students with fewer large-step items, but also required significantly greater training time.

4. "Multiple-choice" students required less training time than "constructed response" students; the two groups did not differ on criterion performance.

The results of the initial experiment, while not definitive, pointed toward an advantage in favor of machine responsiveness over the fixed sequence mode of instruction when training time was taken into consideration. At the same time, experience with the manual devices clearly indicated the desirability of more automatic equipment capable of controlling complex patterns of instructional variables. Project members believed that a computer-based teaching machine would offer maximal responsiveness to individual differences, as well as a high degree of flexibility as an experimental tool.

Before designing a teaching machine with responsiveness to individual differences, however, it was necessary to explore the effects of negative reinforcement in automated teaching.

Since a "responsive" teaching machine uses student errors to determine the sequence of items, it follows that most students will make at least a few errors during each training session. If this were not true, all students would receive the identical sequence. Consequently, an experiment was performed to determine the effects on learning of student errors and resulting negative reinforcement (Melaragno, 1960). Again manual equipment was used, this time to present instructional items in logic to 28 junior-college students. Results indicated that a relatively small number of errors (negative reinforcements) dispersed among correct responses did not affect student learning adversely, but that massed negative reinforcements did hinder learning. The conclusion drawn was that student errors could be used for sequence control in a responsive teaching machine, but that items should be so written that the student would not miss many items in a row.

COMPUTER-BASED TEACHING MACHINE

In early 1960, SDC completed work on an experimental teaching machine consisting of three major units: (1) a Bendix G-15 computer; (2) a random access slide projector; and (3) an electric typewriter.

1. *Bendix G-15 Computer.* This serves as the central control unit for the teaching machine. It contains the master control program which governs the operation of the entire machine. The computer determines, at all times during a training session, what materials are to be presented to the student. It analyzes student responses to the instructional material and compares these responses with stored data.

Rolls of paper tape, each of which can hold the necessary information for a different instructional lesson, are contained in easily interchangeable magazines. A bell mounted in the computer frame can be rung under computer control, thus permitting programmed auditory signals.

2. *Random Access Slide Projector.* Developed by the engineering staff at SDC, this projector holds up to six hundred 35mm slides in 15 magazines of 40 slides each. It receives instructions from the G-15, selecting and projecting instructional slides in the sequence indicated by the computer.

3. *Electric Typewriter.* Two primary functions are served by the typewriter, which is linked to the Bendix computer. First, the student uses the keyboard to insert his answers to the instructional materials, normally in multiple-choice form. Second, the computer program takes control of the typewriter to print messages telling the student how successful he has been in answering the questions.

FUNCTIONAL CHARACTERISTICS OF EXPERIMENTAL MACHINE

The student begins with a "basic series" of items, each of which he attempts to answer in multiple-choice fashion by pressing a key on the typewriter keyboard. He receives appropriate knowledge of results after each attempt. Every item presented to him is registered within the computer control unit as having relevance to one or more specific topics to be taught. The computer keeps a record of the student's performance on each item and a cumulative record of his performance on each of the topics covered by the items. These performance measures may include the student's response times as well as his error count. If student performance falls below a certain level for a particular topic, the student is branched to a special set of items which provide remedial work on that topic. He may be taken through the entire remedial routine, or may be brought more quickly back to the basic series if he performs well on the remedial items.

On returning from the remedial routine the student again receives items from the basic series, continuing until he has finished this series or until his performance once more falls outside certain programmed limits. In the latter case, he is again branched temporarily from the basic series.

In certain cases, a single missed item on a particular topic may be sufficient to take the student to a remedial routine. The teaching machine not only recognizes that an item has been answered incorrectly, but also considers the specific incorrect alternative chosen. Certain answers may be indicative of a serious misunderstanding by the student and may cause the machine to branch immediately to a remedial sequence.

If a student does very poorly in his training and requires excessive remedial work (according to programmed criteria), the machine may take him completely out of the original series, branching him into an alternative basic series. This alternative series represents not simply a remedial routine, but a major change in the training approach. The original series might, for instance, use the procedure of first giving general rules, and then presenting examples to illustrate the rules; the alternative series might reverse the order, gradually building up to a general rule by a progression of illustrative examples.

In the event that a student's performance on some topics of a basic series is sufficiently high, the teaching machine skips certain items for these topics, thereby

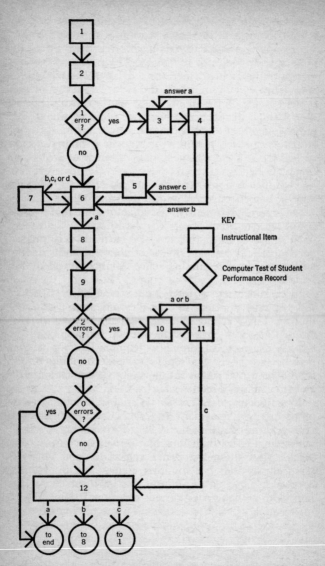

Fig. 1. Flow diagram showing types of decisions which the computer can be programmed to make during a lesson.

212

allowing the brighter student to progress rapidly to more advanced topics.

At various points during the training session the student may be required by the machine to indicate his degree of confidence concerning his own learning progress. If he expresses a feeling of confusion or lack of understanding, he may be taken to a remedial branch even though his actual performance is above the normal criterion level for such a branch. An expression of great self-confidence, on the other hand, may cause the student to be returned more rapidly from a remedial routine to the main sequence.

The operation of the experimental teaching machine may be illustrated by means of the flow chart opposite (Fig. 1). This chart does not represent an actual instructional sequence, but is merely used to demonstrate some of the types of decisions that can be made by a computer-based teaching machine. Each of the numbered squares symbolizes an instructional item. After the student has answered questions in items 1 and 2, the computer determines whether he has missed either question. If he has, the computer gives him remedial items 3 and 4. If not, he goes directly to item 6 (representing a new topic).

On item 4 the correct answer, *b*, takes the student directly to item 6. Answer *a*, representing a particular type of error by the student, causes him to receive item 3 again. Answer *c*, another error, causes him to be given an extra remedial item, 5, before going ahead to item 6.

Item 12 represents a self-evaluation item, in which the student is asked how well he feels he is doing. Answer *a* (e.g., "I think I am doing well and would like to finish now") leads him directly to the end of the lesson. Answer *b* ("I'm doing fine, but I would like some review") takes him to item 8 for a brief review of the materials. Answer *c* ("I don't understand this lesson at all") takes him back to the start of the entire lesson.

EXPERIMENTS COMPLETED

Following the development of the experimental teaching machine, research was started on a number of method variables, task variables, and student variables in automated teaching. The first study (Silberman et al., 1960) investigated the effects of one form of machine responsiveness or branching, using over 400 items in logic. In this study the full capability of the automatic teaching machine was available. Thus a much more elaborate branching procedure was possible than that used in the previous studies with manual equipment.

It was hypothesized that the performance of students receiving a branching sequence would be superior to that of students receiving a fixed sequence, with respect to scores on a criterion post-test. In the branching group a student who had made errors on relatively difficult "main stream" items covering a topic was branched to a longer remedial list of simpler items covering the same topic. It was anticipated that by providing extra remedial items to students who had difficulty, the machine would minimize the number of items seen by the brighter student and the number of errors made by those with low aptitude. The over-all effect was expected to increase the amount of learning in a given time for each individual.

Student aptitude and training time as well as instructional materials were statistically equated for the two groups. With this design, obtained differences could not be attributed to differences in student scholastic aptitude, to amount of study time, nor to the different characteristics of the materials that were presented to the two groups, but only to the responsiveness of the machine to student errors when branching to remedial material.

Mastery of the topics covered by the training items was tested immediately after the training session. Analysis of the test scores yielded no significant difference between the two groups. Several factors indicated that this finding resulted from the particular method of branching used and from the inadequacy of the remedial items. Detailed analysis of item errors showed that the low aptitude students who received remedial materials did not benefit from them since they committed the same kinds of errors on the remedial materials as on main-stream items. The branching procedure also permitted only one trial through the items, so that even if the student still did not understand the topic after completing the remedial items he was sent on to the next topic. In addition, the remedial items differed from the main-stream items only in the size of step or difficulty level, rather than in the approach used to cover the topic.

Another experiment (Melaragno et al., 1960), this one using manual equipment, compared an *optional* branching procedure with the fixed sequence method. Whereas the previous study used branching which depended on student response errors, this study was designed to evaluate a procedure in which the student was allowed to branch at his own discretion. Three groups of high-school seniors were drawn from five schools. The first group received a set of teaching items in fixed sequence. Students in this group read each item in turn and were not permitted to view items already completed. Students in the second group received the same items as those in the first group but were permitted to back up one item at a time and review previous items that had already been covered. The third group received a five-page, single-spaced test consisting of the same materials presented to the other two groups, except that teaching items were cast into statement form and organized into paragraphs. Members of the third group were permitted to branch at their own option either to earlier material or ahead to material not yet covered. Mastery of the topics was tested immediately after the training session. The analysis of test scores showed a significant difference between the optional branching group and the fixed sequence group in favor of branching.

EXPERIMENTS PLANNED

Several experiments are now being planned for 1961. The logic items which were written for the branching-fixed-sequence study are now being revised and the program structure extensively modified for another experimental attack on this problem. The branching decisions will be made not only on the basis of errors but also on the basis of student response time and self-evaluation. If a student takes too much time on certain topics or feels that he needs some review, extra remedial items will be presented to him. A much greater variety of approaches will be used in the remedial items and students will be halted until they have satisfactorily learned each topic.

Another study being planned will not use the computer-controlled machine. One group of students will be required to give overt responses to instructional items presented manually. Students in a second group will receive the same materials, but cast in the form of statements; members of this group will not be required to give an overt response nor permitted to branch among items. A third group will receive the same materials and conditions as the second group except that branching will be encouraged. Learning will be compared for the three conditions. This design is expected to provide some clarification of recent conflicting evidence concerning the relative effectiveness of these methods.

SDC is planning a third project to develop an extensive sequence of items in high school mathematics using the computer-controlled teaching machine. These items will be used in an experiment in a number of high schools to answer certain practical questions concerning the application of auto-instructional methods in the public schools. The study will not be primarily concerned with the general question of whether auto-instructional methods teach, but with a determination of the kinds of students and the kinds of materials for which these methods are most effective. It will use two types of materials: rote and conceptual. The rote material will require specific definitions and memorization of factual detail. The conceptual material will require a progression of thought leading to principles which generalize to novel problem situations. Three kinds of students will be used: over-achievers, normal-achievers, and under-achievers. The results of this study should yield valuable information on methods of applying different self-instructional materials to students of different motivational characteristics. It is expected that when conventional teaching methods are used, over-achievers will perform better than under-achievers on rote materials which have little intrinsic appeal. On the more interesting conceptual topics, little difference is expected between the two groups. When self-instructional materials are used to supplement the regular instruction, it is expected that performance for under-achievers and over-achievers will be essentially equated as the result of elimination of motivational differences between the two groups. This equating of performance is expected for both rote and conceptual materials. The net effect of auto-instruction is expected to be greater for under-achievers than for over-achievers on rote materials, but no different for the two groups on conceptual material.

FUTURE DEVELOPMENTS

The computer-controlled teaching machine presently used at SDC can teach only one student at a time. Plans are now being developed for an expanded facility, using a larger computer control unit, that will give automated instruction to 20 students simultaneously. The same facility will provide automatic storage, analysis, and printout of administrative and counseling data normally associated with an operational school system. Development of the facility will permit the study of important interactions among students, teachers and school administrators.

REFERENCES

COULSON, J. E., and SILBERMAN, H. F., Effects of three variables in a teaching machine, *J. Educ. Psych.*, 1960, **51**, 135-43.

MELARAGNO, R. J., Effects of negative reinforcement in an automated teaching setting, *Psych. Reports*, 1960, **7**, 381-84.

MELARAGNO, R. J., SILBERMAN, H. F., and COULSON, J. F. *A Comparison of Fixed Sequence and Optional Branching Auto-Instructional Methods.* SP-195, System Development Corp., Santa Monica, Calif.; October 1960.

SILBERMAN, H. F., COULSON, J. E., MELARAGNO, R. J., and ESTAVAN, D. P. *Fixed Sequence versus Branching in a Computer-Based Teaching Machine.* SP-213, System Development Corp., Santa Monica, Calif.; November 1960.

15

Teaching Machines and Individual Differences*

ARTHUR R. JENSEN
University of California

In science it is not unusual for a new method or apparatus or technique to give rise to new areas of basic research. At times technical innovations will uncover a realm of phenomena never before accessible to scientific investigation. But, more often a technical development will merely force into greater prominence an already known but perhaps long neglected realm of phenomena. The scientific study of this realm then becomes a necessity if the technical innovation is to realize its full potential in scientific research and ultimately in its application to practical problems.

Such is the case with teaching machines. The recent upsurge of this innovation in educational technology forces us to confront a number of fundamental psychoeducational problems. Of course, the research that first comes to mind with respect to teaching machines is bound to have a practical and technical orientation, dealing with problems of design, programming, the comparative efficiency of teaching various subjects, and so forth. Not far behind these more immediate practical considerations will be some concern with many of the facts, con-

* This article originally appeared in *Automated Teaching Bulletin*, 1960, **1**, 12-17, and is reprinted here with the permission of the author and the editor.

cepts, and theories derived from the experimental psychology of human learning. Thus, teaching machines are of interest not only to the applied psychologist, but also to the psychologist devoted to so-called "pure" or "basic" research on human learning. Most of the interest in teaching machines in academic circles today has been evinced either by experimental psychologists or by educational psychologists who seem to be more interested in the immediate practical applications of teaching machines. So far it appears that differential psychologists, i.e., those concerned with the study of individual differences, have not shown an active interest in teaching machines.

Perhaps because of certain historical accidents in the development of scientific psychology, such as the fact that experimental psychology very early took the physical sciences as its model, the experimental study of human learning and the study of individual differences have developed quite separately. These two fields—experimental psychology and differential psychology—traditionally have left each other pretty much alone. As a result, there is a large and rather clearly defined gap in our psychological knowledge of human behavior. This strange and bewildering gulf in psychology, which continues to persist, has been a detriment to our efforts to gain a greater understanding of human behavior. Now it appears that research on teaching machines may ultimately force a rapprochement between the experimental psychology of learning and the study of individual differences in learning.

The presence of individual differences in school performance are so obviously great as to have become traditionally one of the primary concerns of educational psychology. But nearly all of the efforts to measure individual differences have been what might be called "static." Rather than studying individual differences in the dynamics of behavioral change, we have studied only the end products of learning by means of our intelligence tests, aptitude tests, and achievement tests. How people differ in the processes by means of which behavioral change takes place is truly an unknown and unexplored territory in psychology.

Individual differences in learning will not be overcome or will not suddenly become unimportant when teaching machines are used. In all probability individual differences will be accentuated. The teaching machine, far more effectively than the human teacher, can capitalize on individual differences if they are properly taken into account. I am not referring here only to such gross and obvious individual differences as time or number of trials needed to learn a given quantity of material. There are undoubtedly many other more complex ways in which people differ in learning. For example, there are learning curves for two persons which are almost identical under conditions of distributed practice, but which diverge greatly from each other under conditions of massed practice. Among more or less equally intelligent college students one can observe great individual differences in machine learning under conditions of subject-pacing and of machine-pacing. Some students seem to learn more easily and quickly when they work at their own pace, while others do better when the pace is set by the machine. Our usual intelligence tests and aptitude tests will be of little value in discovering the kinds of individual differences that will increase our understanding of performance on teaching machines. The kinds of learning difficulties that will show up in working with teaching machines will not lend themselves to diagnosis by means of the presently available psychological tests. At present we do not even know what we should measure in order to get a better understanding of how and why various persons differ in their performance on teaching machines. It seems safe to say that individual differences in performance on teaching machines cannot be acounted for merely in terms of a simple unidimensional concept of "intelligence" or "learning ability." Therefore, in order really to understand performance on teaching machines, so that the diagnosis of learning difficulties can be effective and so that in the use of teaching machines subject variables (i.e., individual differences) as well as independent variables (i.e., those controlled by the machine) can be taken into account to achieve maximum efficiency, we must know a great deal about individual differences in learning.

The study of individual differences in learning is important for still another reason. Without such study we cannot properly assess the relative importance of other parameters in learning efficiency, such as schedules of reinforcement, spaced vs. massed practice, stimulus and response similarity, whole vs. part learning, etc. For example, Underwood (1959) has expressed the opinion that the variable of spaced vs. massed practice is probably of little importance as a factor in the efficiency of verbal learning. The basis for this opinion is merely the *average* difference between spaced and massed practice for a large number of subjects. In the experiments on this topic we find that individual differences in learning under spaced and massed practice conditions are treated merely as "error variance," and, interestingly enough, this variance, which is really the "between subjects" variance, is large in proportion to the variance due to experimental variables. This being the case, Underwood's conjecture is not at all convincing. It may well be that some subjects do better and others do worse under massed than under distributed practice, so that only *on the average* does this particular variable appear to be of slight importance. The same thing may be true for many other variables, the effects of which are simply cancelled out when we average a large number of subjects. Obviously what we need is the investigation of what experimental psychologists have always regarded as a nuisance known as "error variance." All of this "error variance" is, of course, not error in the sense of inaccuracy of measurement. Most of it is "between subjects" variance, i.e., variance due to individual differences, and it warrants scientific investigation in its own right.

So far in the history of psychology attempts to discover laws of learning have ignored the individual difference variables. It now seems reasonable to believe that learning theory will have to acknowledge the existence of individual differences if much of the theory is to be applicable to individual cases. "Laws of learning" will have to include statements about individual differences.

Because of this gap in our psychological knowledge, to which recent developments such as the teaching machine have at last forced our attention, the writer has conceived the need for a long-term program of systematic research on individual differences in human learning. This program is already underway in the writer's laboratory.

The first requirements of such a project are of a technological and methodological nature. First of all, a highly standardized experimental procedure for investigating learning variables and measuring performance is needed. For this purpose we are using a specially constructed apparatus which has many points in common with teaching machines. In some ways it is more limited and yet more flexible than a teaching machine need be.

It is essentially three parts: (1) a stimulus display unit, consisting of a screen onto which various stimuli can be projected, (2) a response unit, consisting of a panel of buttons which can be varied in number and position, and (3) a control unit, which consists of (a) a "reader" for the punched tape on which the entire experiment is programmed, (b) a bank of electrical counters which tabulate the subject's performance throughout the course of learning, and (c) "criterion counters" which stop the machine when the subject has attained any set criterion of learning. The rate of stimulus presentation can be either subject-paced or machine-paced.

The apparatus permits trial and error selective learning (the subject is "reinforced" by a tone when he presses the "correct" button corresponding to a particular stimulus), paired-associate learning, serial learning, discrimination learning, probability learning, multiple-choice decision making, and abstract reasoning or problem solving. The stimulus materials are placed inside the stimulus display unit in the form of slides. The order of stimulus presentation and the schedule of reinforcement are programmed on telegraphic tape. Thus, many subjects can be run through an experiment automatically with perfect uniformity of experimental procedure, an important consideration in obtaining reliable measures of individual differences in performance. The subject may respond verbally or by pressing buttons which may be labelled in various ways. The use of buttons makes it possible to clearly define and delimit the subject's response repertoire.

For quite some time it will be necessary to keep our

experiments on a very simple level in terms of the *content* of the learning, since we wish to avoid as much as possible the effects of previous learning which may show up in the form of associations, coding tricks, mnemonic devices, etc. For the same reason, we are using non-verbal stimuli. Students are learning to associate pressing certain buttons in response to such stimuli as squares, circles, and triangles colored red, blue, and yellow. Since at present we are interested only in simple associative learning, the use of such simple, easily discriminable stimuli obviates the need for the student to learn the stimuli themselves as would be the case if we used nonsense syllables. Eventually, of course, it will become desirable to use more complex stimuli and to introduce verbal materials. One advantage of the present set-up is that it permits the experimenter to perform a great variety of learning experiments all of which still involve essentially the same experimental parameters. He can change one variable at a time while all others are held constant. Thus a continuity and integration of findings from many different experiments will be possible. This is a most important feature as our research is envisaged as a very long-term program.

What is the underlying plan or "philosophy" of this research program? It may be considered an attempt to discover the basic dimensions underlying individual differences in various learning phenomena, much as differential psychologists have sought to discover the dimensions underlying cognitive abilities or personality characteristics. Since learning depends upon the nervous system, a product of biological evolution, it seems safe to assume that there is a limit to the number of ways in which people differ in the learning process. That is, there should be a limited number of fundamental dimensions in terms of which individual differences in various kinds of learning may be described. It seems most unlikely that there should be no "structure" to learning ability in the human species, since such structure is to be found in every other natural biological function. It is assumed that the capacity for learning is one such biological function.

The investigator need not blindly begin his search for these dimensions. Learning theory, especially that deriving from Clark Hull, offers us some clues as to the possible nature of the dimensions we might discover. For example, individual differences in performance on learning tasks might be thought of as a joint effect of individual variations in such Hullian variables as habit strength (ease of formation of associations), drive strength, inhibition (a function of effortfulness of response, repetition, and non-reinforcement), and so on. For example, differences in habit strength may show up in terms of sheer speed of learning when subjects are equated on other variables. Differences in inhibition may show up in rate of extinction, in differential rates of learning under massed and spaced practice, and in the magnitude of reminiscence effects. At present we have no idea how many basic dimensions we will ultimately find. One may hypothesize, for example, a dimension of susceptibility to "interference" or response competition which would be expected to show up in experiments on proactive and retroactive inhibition and associative interference. On the other hand, individual differences in these "interference" phenomena may be derived from more fundamental dimensions, perhaps, for example, from an interaction between habit strength and drive. These are the kinds of problems we are setting out to study.

Another problem on which sooner or later large-scale research will have to be launched concerns the relation between acquisition and retention. It may be that the dimensions we discover underlying individual differences in learning or acquisition will not be the same as those involved in the long-term retention of what has been learned.

The specific plan of research consists first of determining, within the confines of our simple experimental set-up, the extent or degree of individual differences existing in various learning phenomena: simple selective learning, extinction, reminiscence, learning under different degrees of task complexity, reinforcement schedules, distributed vs. massed practice, whole vs. part learning, stimulus and response generalization, transfer, retention, "learning to learn," and "interference" phenomena such as proactive and retroactive inhibition and associative interference. It is necessary to determine the reliability of measurement of individual differences on these phenomena. This usually involves testing the same subjects at least twice on equivalent forms of the learning task. The "dimensions" within this limited set of phenomena would be, we hope, teased out by means of factor analysis or some other appropriate form of multivariate analysis.

Next we would explore the generality of these dimensions in other forms of learning than simple selective trial and error learning, e.g., paired associate learning and serial learning, still keeping the learning content relatively simple. We would hope that the dimensions thus discovered in our simple, rigorous, and highly controlled laboratory experiments could later be reliably measured in individuals and could be identified in their performance under the less simple and less rigorous conditions approximating those found in the practical use of teaching machines. First in this wilderness we must seek the basic dimensions in the most simple and "purified" forms of various learning phenomena. What is discovered and proved in the laboratory may later be demonstrated in more gross practical situations.

Still quite far in the future in regard to the work planned for the writer's laboratory is a third stage of this research. It will consist of relating the dimensions of learning to the factors already discovered in the realm of intellectual or cognitive abilities and in the personality domain.

We cannot extrapolate too far ahead, for we are just at the beginning in this research. It is hard to tell in advance just where our findings will next lead us. For certain practical reasons, that are not very logical in terms of our over-all program as outlined here, individual differences in serial learning and in the bowing of the serial position curve so far have received the greater part of our efforts. Also, some interesting linkages between individual differences in serial learning phenomena in the laboratory and *spelling* in school have been discovered which suggest that learning to spell may be considered, at least in part, as a problem of serial learning. Linkages between other laboratory learning phenomena and other forms of school learning are being sought, so that the work of our laboratory is not completely divorced from practical problems of learning.

It is hoped that eventually in the not too distant future a truly scientific and practically fruitful rapprochment will be achieved between learning theory, the experimental psychology of human learning, differential psychology, the psychology of school subjects, and the applied technology of teaching machines.

REFERENCE

UNDERWOOD, B. J., Verbal Learning in the Educative Processes, *Harvard Educational Review*, 1959, **29**, 107-117.

16

Programmed Self-Instruction: Possibilities and Limitations*

GENE C. FUSCO

School Administration Branch,
U.S. Office of Education

POSSIBILITIES

Proponents of programmed self-instruction maintain that this is not a new method of teaching; the basic procedure is found as far back as the Socratic dialogue. What is new, they say, is the development of a science and a technology based on a method employed by the great teachers of the past. Thus, some aspects of the art of teaching may become a part of the science of learning through programmed self-instruction.

Theoretically, the mechanical tutors represent labor-saving devices for the teacher since the self-instructional techniques are tailored to the learning speed of the individual student. This method provides the student with as much practice as he needs, permits the rapid learner to cover the material quickly and the slower student to proceed at his own pace. As a consequence, the classroom teacher may be freed from the burdensome and time-consuming tasks of *presenting* material and taking pre-

---

* This article is an abridgement of a paper which originally appeared in *The High School Journal*, 1960, **59**, 85-90. It is used here with the permission of the author and the editor.

cious class time to repeat material for students who didn't get it the first time.

Advocates of self-instructional techniques further maintain that this method may be adapted to home study and can save the teacher from devoting time to the correction of individual assignments. Self-correcting homework materials, it may be noted, have been prepared in high school English by Educational Testing Service (Diederich, 1960). Self-instructional materials may also be used by temporarily homebound students who may keep up with assignments while unable to attend regularly scheduled classes. In addition, some propose that programmed materials may be used in small high schools with limited curriculum offerings to meet the needs of students who request courses not included in the school program.

Students working with self-instructional materials will be enabled to work privately and independently and, as a consequence, recognize the fruits of their own labor. It is contended that this will result in a lessening of invidious comparisons of their achievements with that of their classmates.

According to Simon Ramo, in the high school of the future there will still be human teachers and classroom sessions, but each student will spend a large proportion of each day interacting with computer-controlled teaching machines. The machines will tutor the student, schedule the curriculum to suit his individual abilities, and provide his human teachers with a detailed description of his academic strengths and weaknesses. Ramo foresees the need for highly skilled teachers who can work closely with subject matter specialists and "teaching engineers" in modifying and revising the teaching devices and programs (Ramo, 1957).

LIMITATIONS

There are now dozens of different types of devices that could be classified as teaching machines, most of which represent minor variations of two, or at best, three or four basic designs. At present, good problem materials to be used with teaching machines, and procedures and principles for the preparation of such materials have not kept pace with the development of the devices themselves. There is a lack of extensive empirical data on the effectiveness of this method of teaching. Despite some favorable findings of research in self-instructional techniques, there is little evidence on the factors that make that particular machine design or set of instructional items effective. There is much to be learned about the preparation of good items, and there are hardly any criteria to determine whether the items in a program are "good."

Another limitation is that the selection of a particular teaching machine places severe limitations on the type of variables the researcher can investigate. Teaching machines, for the most part, are single-purpose devices with limited adaptability. Thus, it is possible for the machine to dictate the direction of research, whereas, ideally, research considerations should direct the development of the machine.

Another problem in reference to the inflexibility of programmed self-instructional methods is that a particular program may not be optimally effective for all members of a typical class. Students, after all, differ in both experience and in inherent ability, or "intelligence." An "ideal" sequence of items for one student may be less effective for some other student.

Teaching machines present items in an essentially predetermined sequence, permit the student to respond, and give him immediate feedback. But does the fact that a student is shown the correct answer, or selects the correct answer after several attempts, insure that he has actually acquired knowledge? The machine does not "know" whether the student has mastered the material the way a human instructor may know through observation and questioning.

Professor Skinner, for example, insists that a student through machine instruction will be enabled to proceed at his own level, advancing as rapidly as he can. Under these conditions, he says, the conventional grading system will have to be overhauled since a grade will be useful only in showing *how far* a student has gone. Thus, a "C" might mean that he is halfway through a course.

Given enough time, says Skinner, he can achieve an "A."

In challenging Skinner's point of view, one psychologist calls attention to the question of transfer and cites studies on overlearning which tend to show that performance may not mirror how much has been learned. He questions whether the completion of a programmed course is the final criterion of learning (Kendlar, 1959).

Other limitations of programmed instruction include the large expenditure of money, the great amount of time, and the application of special skills necessary to produce a program; the difficulty of determining the specific body of knowledge to be programmed; and the fact that the method lacks a philosophy of application in the instructional process.

REFERENCES

DIEDERICH, P. B., The Rutgers plan for cutting class size in two, *The English Journal*, 1960, **49**, No. 4.

RAMO, SIMON, A new technique of education, *Engineering and Science*, 1957, **21** (October).

KENDLER, H. H., Teaching machines and psychological theory. In Eugene Galanter (Ed.). *Automatic Teaching: The State of the Art*. New York: Wiley, 1959.

Appendix A

Teaching Machine Terms: A Glossary*

Desmond L. Cook

Purdue University

In compiling this glossary, the author drew from several sources in addition to his own experience and acquaintance with the area of "teaching machines." The primary references were Eugene Galanter, *Automatic Teaching: The State of the Art* (John Wiley, 1959); William Carr, *Self-Instructional Devices: A Review of Current Concepts,* Wright Air Development Center, Technical Report 59-503, August 1959; and Edward Fry, Glenn Bryan, and Joseph Rigney, "Teaching Machines: An Annotated Bibliography," *AV Communication Review,* Vol. 8, No. 2 (Supplement 1), 1960.

Unpublished papers and reports, personal correspondence, and comments received on the first draft from persons actively engaged in research in the area were also utilized. Some terms were secured from a similar draft glossary prepared by Charles Darby, Department of Psychology, Purdue University.

Augmenting. One way in which guidance through a program is created is by augmenting, or introducing bits of information that will lead the student into a new concept.

Auto-instructional methods. A comprehensive term suggested

* This article originally appeared in *Audiovisual Instruction*, 1961, **6**, 152-153, and is used here with permission of the author and the publisher.

by Lunsdaine and Klaus to describe instruction characterized by the controlled presentation of material, the elicitation of appropriate response, guidance with respect to the subject matter, and control of the way in which learning proceeds.

Automated instruction. Instructional methods considered generally to comprehend any means, devices or material, whereby teacher or tutor functions (actual or desirable) are replaced, or provided, by a wholly or partially automated sequence of instructional segments that is prepared in advance and is capable of instructing effectively when presented without direct intervention or modification by a teacher. Also called "automatic teaching."

Automatic teaching. See "*Automated instruction.*"

Automatic tutoring. An individual instructorless method of teaching which is an automation of the classical process of individual tutoring.

Choice. Refers to the selection of an answer from several alternatives presented to the subject as opposed to having the subject construct or write out an answer.

Construction. The process of requiring the subject to write out or prepare an answer as opposed to choosing one of several alternative answers.

Confirming mechanism. A device or means by which the student has his response confirmed as being right or wrong. Correctness or error can be indicated through the presentation of visual or auditory signals, or, in the case of constructive answers, the presentation of the correct or model answers.

Conversational chaining. A term introduced by Barlow to describe a program wherein the movement from item to item follows less the question-answer pairs in other programs and more the natural train of conversation so that the lesson becomes the main unit of concern for the student rather than the item.

Cue, vanishing. A prompt presented originally, but gradually reduced or eliminated, thereby requiring the student to provide the responses independently.

Display mechanism. The mechanical means by which the programmed set of materials is presented visually or aurally to the subject.

Error. An incorrect or non-appropriate answer to a specific item in the program.

Error rate. Refers to the number or percentage of a given group of subjects incorrectly responding to a specific item on the program. A high degree of error would probably indicate a need for revision in the program.

Fading. The gradual withdrawal of stimulus support in presenting items.

Feedback. Communicating to the subject pursuing a sequence of programmed materials the information needed to modify responses so that failures or errors can be eliminated and correct responses maintained.

Frame. A single item or statement is exposed at a time. The exposed material constitutes a single frame.

Frame, forced. A stimulus frame presented to the student forcing him to respond correctly by obvious nature of the answer.

Frame, response. That part of a teaching machine or programmed textbook which permits the subject to record his response to the item presented by means of the stimulus frame. (See stimulus frame.)

Frame, stimulus. That part of a mechanical teaching machine or programmed textbook containing the individual items, in the form of a question or statement, to which the student is to respond. Also refers to the mechanical part of the teaching machine which allows the examinee to see the item.

Hints. Devices used to direct the students' behavior in the desired direction. Used to increase the likelihood of a correct response.

Item, augmenting. An item supplying new information but not requiring the student to make a relevant response.

Item, delayed review. An item which allows for the distribution of practice. Differs from other items only in terms of presentation.

Item, dovetailing. An item requiring the student to make separate responses to separate stimuli which otherwise may become confused.

Item, fading. An item requiring the student to review what has been presented. In addition the item withdraws information successively. Similar to Skinner's "vanishing technique."

Item, generalizing. An item presenting a verbal statement pointing to a common characteristic of several specific problems already presented to the subject.

Item, interlocking. An item that requires a student to review the established skills while new information is being presented.

Item, lead in. An item not requiring new information or rehearsal of old skills but functions to orient the subject to a problem and prepare him for new information.

Item, restated review. An item requiring a rehearsal of the skill where a problem is restated.

Item, rote review. An item presenting a problem identical to one presented earlier.

Item, specifying. An item which exemplifies a general rule or principle.

Item, subject matter. An item classified with respect to its subject matter content.

Item, tab. A specialized term referring to having the subject pull a tab to indicate his response rather than writing out an answer or selecting a choice.

Leading. The student is first asked to talk about familiar things using his everyday vocabulary. He is then led to discuss relations among these. Technical terms are then slowly inserted.

Learning machine. A term often applied to teaching machines. An inappropriate term for describing a mechanical teaching device since it implies that a machine learns.

Matching. Procedure used in some Skinner machines to inform student of correctness of his response. After writing his response, the student moves a lever which exposes the correct answer with which the student compares or "matches" his response.

Operant behavior. Behavior which operates or acts upon the environment. A fundamental concept in Skinnerian learning theory.

Pace. The rate at which the subject is permitted to work through the programmed material.

Pacing, controlled rate. Control of the subjects' rate of responding by features of the mechanical device utilized to present the program.

Pacing, self. The rate at which the subject might complete the material at his own rate depending upon success on the previous steps.

Panel. A short passage of prose material, graphs, and similar material which are presented or studied along with the discs in the Skinner device.

Paper teaching machine. Refers to the "scrambled" or "programmed" textbook type of self-instructional devices.

Porter device. A device similar to the Skinner disc machine, except instead of using round discs, a regular sheet of paper is inserted into the mechanism. The paper contains the programmed material and spaces for insertion of answers.

Pressey device. The earliest known device (1926) originally developed for use with multiple choice tests. Device could be set so that items missed could be skipped or repeated until success was established, a raw score obtained, and an item analysis or error count secured.

Program. The subject matter that is to be learned by the student via the machine or other device.

Programmed book. A special book in which the subject matter to be learned has been arranged into a series of sequential steps leading from familiar concepts to new materials. Differs from a "scrambled textbook" in that the content is arranged so that the student proceeds directly from one step to the next, or one succeeding page to the next, rather than skipping around. The student generally is asked to construct a response as opposed to choice.

Programmed learning. A term sometimes used synonymously to refer to the broader concept of "auto-instructional methods."

Programmer. Generally, a curriculum specialist who subdivides the material to be learned into the sequential steps for later use with the mechanical method of presenting the program.

Programming. The process of arranging the material to be learned into a series of sequential steps; usually moves the student from a familiar background into a complex and new set of concepts, principles, and understandings.

Programming, intrinsic. A method of programming materials that directs the erring subject along certain corrective pathways before he is permitted to proceed to the next step in the program. Requires that each step contain multiple choice answers.

Prompt. Some type of verbal or symbolic cue which facilitates the desired response from the subject.

Prompting. The method or sequence of providing verbal and symbolic cues to encourage responses. Can be visual, verbal, symbolic, or auditory.

Reinforcement, immediate. The process of providing the subject with immediate feedback or information regarding the success or failure of his performance.

Reinforcement mechanism. Some type of reward for responding correctly to the items in the display. A motivational factor causing the individual to keep working at the set of materials. Sometimes considered as an integral part of the confirming mechanism.

Reinforcer, immediate. A self-instructional aid which contains a built-in system of providing the student with immediate knowledge of the success or failure of his performance.

Response device. A type of teaching aid which permits the student to practice certain types of responses. No stimulus is presented as part of this type of device.

Response mechanism. A device which permits the student to record his response to the items presented in the display mechanism. Usually is either the selection of one of several choices or writing an answer to the item in the program.

Response mode. The form of the response a student makes while working on a program.

Scrambled book. A special book containing material to be learned in programmed sequential form, but in which the student is directed to different pages not necessarily in consecutive order. By means of alternate choice responses at each step, branching to new or review material is made possible.

Self-instructional device. A mechanical or paper device which presents a set of planned sequential materials to be learned and which the student can complete in the absence of a live instructor and at his own rate of speed.

Shaping. The building of a behavior or set of behaviors through the differential reinforcement of progressively more adequate forms of behavior. (Skinner)

Skinner device. A mechanical device which presents a set of programmed materials. At each step the subject must construct an answer and evaluate its correctness with a model answer before proceeding further in the program. Generally considered the forerunner of later model "teaching machines."

Skinner disc. A round, flat, record-like device which contains a set or series of program materials for the Skinner device. Contains the questions to be answered, spaces for recording student's answers and the correct response, as well as for making a record of successful or unsuccessful performance.

Step. The increment in subject matter level to be learned with each succeeding item or frame in the program.

Step size. The amount of increase in subject matter difficulty with each step in the program. A large step size could result in relatively few frames while a low step would indicate a relatively large number of frames in the program.

Stimulus device. A type of teaching aid which presents materials to the subject through one or several of the various senses. No active response is required on the part of the subject during the presentation of the materials.

Stimulus-response device. A teaching aid which not only presents material to the subject through any or several of the various senses, but also requires a response to the stimulus presented in order to progress further in the program of instruction.

Terminal behavior. The behavior a program is designed to produce.

Track, multiple. A provision within the programmed material for allowing subjects to pursue alternative subdivisions of the program in terms of their successes or failures with earlier sections of the sequence.

Track, single. A common set of programmed materials which all subjects work through, there being no alternative program such as in the multiple track situation.

Vanishing. The basic problem here is to evoke a given bit of behavior, at least once, in the presence of an appropriate stimulus, so that it can be reinforced. One solution is to begin with stimuli which already control the behavior and to reduce them slowly as learning proceeds.

Appendix B

1. Additional Sources of Information on Programmed Instruction

BOOKS

GALANTER, EUGENE (Ed.). *Automatic Teaching: The State of the Art.* New York: Wiley, 1959.

LUMSDAINE, A. A., and GLASER, ROBERT (Eds.). *Teaching Machines and Programmed Learning: A Source Book.* Washington, D.C.: Natl. Educ. Assn., 1960 (724 pp.).

PERIODICALS CARRYING RELEVANT
ARTICLES REGULARLY

AID, Institute of International Research and Development
  Educational and Training Methods Division
  Box 4456, Lubbock, Texas

Audio-Visual Communication Review, Department of Audiovisual
  Instruction, National Education Association
  1201 Sixteenth Street, N.W.
  Washington 6, D.C.

Contemporary Psychology, American Psychological Association
  1313 Sixteenth Street
  Washington 6, D.C.

Programed Instruction, The Center for Programed Instruction, Inc.
  365 West End Avenue
  New York 24, New York

The Automated Teaching Bulletin, Rheem Califone Corporation
  1020 North LaBrea Avenue
  Los Angeles 38, California

PERIODICALS CARRYING RELEVANT
ARTICLES IRREGULARLY*

Audiovisual Instruction, Department of Audiovisual Instruction
    National Education Association
    1201 Sixteenth Street, N.W.
    Washington 6, D.C.
Harvard Educational Review, Harvard University
    Cambridge 38, Massachusetts
Journal of Educational Psychology, The American Psychological Association, Inc., 1333 Sixteenth Street, N.W.
    Washington 6, D.C.
Journal of Experimental Analysis of Behavior, Psychology Department
    Indiana University
    Bloomington, Indiana
Journal of Psychology, The Journal Press
    2 Commercial Street
    Provincetown, Massachusetts
Phi Delta Kappan, Eighth and Union Avenue,
    Bloomington, Indiana
Psychological Reports, Southern Universities Press
    Box 1441,
    Missoula, Montana

2. Manufacturers of Teaching Machines*

Astra Corporation, 31 Church Street, New London, Connecticut

Deveraux Teaching Aids, Smith-Harrison, Inc., Box 717
717 Devon, Pennsylvania

Dyna-Slide Company, 600 South Michigan, Chicago 5, Illinois

Foringer and Co., Inc., 312 Maple Drive, Rockville, Maryland

General Atronics Corporation, 1 Bala Avenue, Bala-Cynwyd, Pennsylvania

Hamilton Research Associates, Inc., Box 38, New Hartford, New York

Hughes Aircraft Company, Industrial Systems Division, Box 90904 Airport Station, Los Angeles 45, California

Koncept-O-Graph Corporation, Box 533, Rochester 3, New York

Management Research Associates, 185 North Wabash, Chicago, Illinois

* A partial list.

Programmed Teaching Aids, Inc., 3810 South Four Mile
Run Drive, Arlington, Virginia

Rheem Califone Corporation, 1020 North LaBrea Avenue,
Los Angeles 38, California

Western Design, U.S. Industries, Inc., Santa Barbara, California

3. Sources of Programs*

Doubleday and Company, Inc., 501 Franklin Avenue, Gar-
den City, New York, *Tutor Texts*

Harcourt, Brace and World, Inc., 730 Third Avenue, New
York 17, New York

Institute of International Research and Development, Educational and Training Methods Division, Box 4456, Lubbock, Texas

McGraw-Hill Book Company, Inc., College Department, 330
West Forty-Second Street, New York 36, New York

Programmed Learning Materials, Encyclopaedia Britannica
Films, Inc., 1150 Wilmette Avenue, Wilmette, Illinois

Science Research Associates, Inc., 259 East Erie Street, Chicago 11, Illinois

Student Self-Instruction Project, Earlham College, Rich-
mond, Indiana

TMI-Grolier, 235 San Pedro Drive, N.E., Albuquerque, New
Mexico

The Center for Programmed Instruction, 365 West End
Avenue, New York 24, New York

* A partial list.